TALK
JAPANESE
GAMBATTE!

TALK
JAPANESE
GAMBATTE!

にほんごがんばって！

Kazuhiko Nagatomo

Kodansha International
Tokyo · New York · London

Gambatte! means to "hang on in there" and "not to give up." All titles in this series include the word *Gambatte!* as we would like to offer our encouragement to learners of all ages who have decided for whatever reason to study a language as difficult as Japanese. Good luck and *Gambatte!*

Talk Japanese Gambatte! is based upon "Nihongo Shokyu: Beginning Japanese" which was originally serialized in *The Nihongo Journal* (published by ALC Press Inc.) between April 1992 and March 1993.

Kazuhiko Nagatomo is Professor of Japanese Language and Culture at Ochanomizu University, Tokyo

Published by Kodansha International Ltd., 17-14, Otowa 1-chome, Bunkyo-ku, Tokyo 112 and Kodansha America Inc. Distributed in the United States by Kodansha America, Inc., 114, Fifth Avenue, New York, New York 10011, and in the United Kingdom and continental Europe by Kodansha Europe Ltd., 95 Aldwych, London WC2B 4JF.

First edition, 1995
95 96 97 98 10 9 8 7 6 5 4 3 2 1

ISBN 4-7700-1932-7

Designed by Adachi Office
Edited by Guild
Printed in Japan by Dai-Nippon Printing Company

Library of Congress cataloging in publication data available

CONTENTS

How to Use This Book —— 7

Main Grammatical Features of Each Unit —— 8

❶ 花見 Flower-viewing —— 9

❷ ゴールデンウィーク Golden Week —— 17

❸ 結婚式 Wedding —— 27

❹ たなばた Tanabata —— 37

❺ 夏休み Summer Holiday —— 47

❻ 月見と台風 Moon-viewing and Typhoons —— 57

❼ スポーツ Sports —— 67

❽ 紅葉 Autumn Colors —— 77

❾ クリスマス Christmas —— 87

❿ 正月 New Year's Day —— 97

⓫ 節分 Setsubun —— 107

⓬ 卒業 Graduation —— 117

Answers —— 127

HOW TO USE THIS BOOK

Desinged so that you can acquire basic Japanese through step-by-step and fun method, *Talk Japanese Gambatte!* is aimed at beginners familiar with *hiragana*, *katakana*, numbers, and some simple expressions such as greetings.

The book consists of twelve units, each divided into nine sections: Main Text, Pronunciation (for the Main Text), Explanation (for the Main Text), Dialogue, Pronunciation (for the Dialogue), Explanation (for the Dialogue), Grammar Notes, Drills, and Tasks. These sections are connected by an arrow [→] to guide you to full understanding of the unit. The arrow also helps you to refer to Grammar Notes in the previous units so that you can review what has already been introduced. It is possible to start or review from any unit, but we suggest you start from Unit One and move on to the next at first.

Main Text
The Main Text is given in a plain written style and introduces a topic related to Japanese customs or lifestyle, as well as new sentence structures. You will enjoy a year-round cultural trip through the twelve carefully chosen topics.

Pronunciation
Read aloud repeatedly while paying attention to stress and the signs denoting pitch. In order to perfect your grasp of the characteristics of Japanese pronunciation, you should listen to the tape and try to reproduce what you hear.

Explanation
Often guiding you to the Grammar Notes by an arrow, the Explanation offers a full account of every word, phrase, or sentence in the Main Text and Dialogue.

Dialogue
The Dialogue, given mainly in a polite style, introduces a variety of natural expressions used in everyday conversation. We suggest you to practice these expressions (with fellow group members, if possible) until you can reproduce them without further reference to the Dialogue. For more effective language learning, listen repeatedly to the same dialogue on the cassette tape (available separately from book stores or directly from the publisher.)

Grammar Notes
This is concise explanations of new grammatical items introduced in each unit. The grammatical items, integrated step-by-step throughout the book, cover basic Japanese grammar to help you to gain a good command of Japanese.

Drills
Drills comprise practice questions relating mainly to the Grammar Notes. You can refer to the Grammar Notes as indicated by an arrow and, if necessary, to the answers at the back of the book when attempting the Drills.

Tasks
This is a diverse selection of task-based applied activities you should tackle by referring to the Grammar Notes as the arrow indicates, using the Japanese knowledge you have previously gained. All vocabulary appears at the end of the unit or somewhere in the same unit.

MAIN GRAMMATICAL FEATURES OF EACH UNIT

Unit	Main Grammatical Features
1	●Plain vs. polite forms ●な -adjective and い-adjective ●Demonstratives: これ(この)、それ(その)、あれ(あの)、どれ(どの) ●Basic sentence patterns: (1) 〜は 〜だ／です／0 (2) 〜に 〜が ある／あります (〜は 〜に ある／あります) (3) 〜に 〜が いる／います (〜は 〜に いる／います)
2	●Basic sentence patterns: (1) 〜が／は (〜に) 〜を verb (2) 〜が／は (〜と) 〜へ verb ●Plain/polite affirmative vs. plain/polite negative forms ●All-exclusive expressions: an interogative + も with a negative
3	●Past tenses ●Conjunction particle が
4	●The て／で-form + いる／います to indicate an action in progress or a state of being ●The て／で-form + ある／あります to indicate a state resulting from an action
5	●Comparative sentences
6	●"Hearsay" and "conjecture" expressions with そうだ／そうです
7	●な -adjectives used with particle が ●〜たい／たいです and ほしい／ほしいです desiderative expressions
8	●つもり だ／です and the -[y]oo form to express one's intention ●Quotation particles と／って
9	●Giving and receiving verbs
10	●Conditionals: たら／だら, なら, と, and (れ)ば ●Obligation: 〜なければ ならない／なりません ●Permission: 〜ても／でも いい／いいです ●Prohibition: 〜ては／では いけない／いけません ●Suggestion: 〜た／だ ほうが いい／いいです
11	●Passive, causative, and causative-passive forms
12	●Honorific and humble forms

❶花見
はなみ
Flower-viewing

The springtime custom of *hanami,* or flower-viewing parties, began
with court aristocrats in the 8th century
and spread to everyday people in the 1600s.
A time to ponder the brevity of life and beauty symbolized
by the short-lived cherry blossoms,
today's often rowdy gatherings are also a good excuse for
daytime drinking and *karaoke* singing!
While TV newscasters give regular reports on the
best times and places for flower-viewing,
office juniors scramble to local parks and riversides
to bag a spot for the office *hanami.*
In Tokyo, Ueno Park and the Sumida river are
good places to join hundreds of workers, friends and families picnicking
and downing beer and sake under the blooming cherry trees.

MAIN TEXT — ほんぶん

Read the following passage. If you have fully understood the passage, you shouldn't be studying this course. If not, you are WELCOME to study with us!

花見
<ruby>花<rt>は</rt>見<rt>な み</rt></ruby>

いま <ruby>季節<rt>き せつ</rt></ruby>は <ruby>春<rt>はる</rt></ruby>だ。 <ruby>春<rt>はる</rt></ruby>は <ruby>花見<rt>はな み</rt></ruby>の シーズンだ。 <ruby>公園<rt>こうえん</rt></ruby>に <ruby>大<rt>おお</rt></ruby>きい <ruby>桜<rt>さく ら</rt></ruby>の <ruby>木<rt>き</rt></ruby>が たくさん ある。 <ruby>花見<rt>はな み</rt></ruby>の <ruby>人<rt>ひと</rt></ruby>が たくさん いる。 <ruby>桜<rt>さく ら</rt></ruby>の <ruby>花<rt>はな</rt></ruby>は ほんとうに きれいだ。

Flower-viewing

It's spring now, the season for flower-viewing. The park has lots of big cherry trees, and many people have come to see the blossoms. Cherry flowers are really lovely.

PRONUNCIATION はつおん

Listen to and repeat after the tape. High and low pitches are marked with ⌐ and ⌐, and the stressed word is in bold below.

Ima kisetsu-wa **haru**-da. Haru-wa **hanami**-no shiizun-da. Kooen-ni ookii sakura-no ki-ga **takusan** aru. Hanami-no hito-ga **takusan** iru. Sakura-no hana-wa **hontooni** kiree-da.

EXPLANATION せつめい

The following breakdown of terms will help you to understand the passage.

① 花見

はなみ flower [cherry blossoms] viewing

② いま　季節は　春だ。

いま now

きせつ season

は as for, speaking of: particle [marker] to indicate a topic in the sentence 【→GN(Grammar Notes)❶-4】

はる spring

だ is, are: copula; basic plain [dictionary] form 【→GN ❶-1, 4】

③ 春は　花見の　シーズンだ。

の particle to indicate the noun that modifies a succeeding noun

シーズン season

④ 公園に　大きい　桜の　木が　たくさん　ある。

こうえん park

に a location particle 【→GN❶-4】

おおきい big: い-adjective 【→GN❶-2】

さくら cherry blossoms

き tree

が particle to indicate the subject, i.e., what is being talked about in the sentence 【→GN❶-4】

たくさん many

ある there is, there are: an existential verb [here, in the plain form] used when the subject is inanimate 【→GN❶-4】

⑤花見の　人が　たくさん　いる。

ひと person
いる there is, there are: an existential verb [here, in the
　　plain form] used when the subject is animate【→

GN **❶**-4】

⑥桜の　花は　ほんとうに　きれいだ。

ほんとうに really, truly
きれい pretty, attractive: な-adjective【→GN**❶**-1, 4】

DIALOGUE — かいわ

Did you understand the passage? If you did, please imagine that you are under beautiful cherry blossoms with your friend. You might have a conversation like the following:

陳　：たくさん　人が　いますね。

金田：ええ、にぎやかですね。　でも、カラオケは　すこし　うるさい
　　　ですね。

陳　：そうですね。　木村さんたちは　どこに　いますか。

金田：ほら、あそこです。

陳　：ああ、あの　大きい　木の　そばですね。

金田：ええ。　中国にも　お花見の　しゅうかんが　ありますか。

陳　：いいえ、ありません。　でも、中国の　桜も　きれいですよ。

Chen : There are lots of people here, aren't there?
Kaneda : Yes–isn't it lively? The *karaoke* is a bit loud, though.
Chen : Yes, it is. Where are Mr. Kimura and the others?
Kaneda : Look, they're over there.
Chen : Oh yes, next to that big tree.
Kaneda : Do you have a flower-viewing tradition in China too?
Chen : No, we don't. But the cherry blossoms in China are very nice anyway.

Listen to and repeat after the tape. Try to imitate well when practicing this exercise.

Chen : **Takusan** hito-ga imasu-ne.

Kaneda : Ee, **nigiyaka**-desu-ne. Demo, karaoke-wa sukoshi **urusai**-desu-ne.

Chen : **Soo**-desu-ne. **Kimura**-san-tachi-wa doko-ni imasu-ka.

Kaneda : Hora, **asoko**-desu.

Chen : Aa, ano ookii ki-no **soba**-desu-ne.

Kaneda : Ee. **Chuugoku**-ni-mo o-hanami-no shuukan-ga arimasu-ka.

Chen : Iie, **arimasen**. Demo, Chuugoku-no sakura-mo **kiree**-desu-yo.

EXPLANATION　せつめい

Did you understand the dialogue? If you didn't, the following breakdown of terms will help you to understand and enjoy it.

⑦ たくさん　人が　いますね。

います there is, there are: the polite form of いる above
　【→GN❶-1, 4】
ね isn't it true!: particle used at the end of a sentence for
　confirmation or exclamation

⑧ ええ、にぎやかですね。

ええ Yes: more informal than はい
にぎやか lively: な-adjective
です is, are: the polite form of the copula だ 【→GN❶-
1, 4】

⑨ でも、カラオケは　すこし
　うるさいですね。

でも but: conjunction, more informal than しかし
カラオケ *karaoke* music
すこし a little, a few
うるさい noisy: い-adjective

⑩ そうですね。木村さんたちは どこに
　いますか。

そうですね That's right/Yes, isn't it?
きむらさん Mr. Kimura
たち and the others: plural suffix
どこ where 【→GN❶-4】
か particle to make a sentence into a question

⑪ ほら、あそこです。

ほら Look!, There!
あそこ that place over there 【→GN❶-4】

⑫ ああ、あの　大きい　木の　そば
　ですね。

ああ Ah!, Oh!
あの that ＿ over there 【→GN❶-3】
そば next to

⑬ ええ。中国にも　お花見の
　しゅうかんが　ありますか。

ちゅうごく China
も also
お prefix to make はなみ a more polite expression
しゅうかん custom, habit
あります there is, there are: the polite form of ある
　【→GN❶-1, 4】

⑭ いいえ、ありません。でも、中国の
　桜も　きれいですよ。

いいえ no
ありません there is not, there are not: the negative
　form of あります
よ particle used at the end of a sentence for emphasis

GRAMMAR NOTES (GN❶)
ぶんぽうノート

【GN❶-1】

The polite forms should be used when you are expected to be polite to the listener. Otherwise, the basic plain forms (the affirmative forms of which appear in the dictionary) may be used.

	Noun	な-adjective	い-adjective	existential verb	
plain form	はるだ	にぎやかだ	うるさい	ある	いる
polite form	はるです	にぎやかです	うるさいです	あります	います

※うるさいだ is ungrammatical! 　　　　　　　　　　　　　　　　　　　　　　　【→ Drill, Task 1, 2】

【GN❶-2】

な-adjectives are adjectival nouns which modify nouns with な attached to them, and い-adjectives are い-ending adjectives which modify nouns as they are.

```
な-adjective：にぎやかな　まち　　（lively town）
　　　　　　　きれいな　はな　　　（pretty flower）
　　　　　　　すてきな　へや　　　（wonderful room）
い-adjective：うるさい　おと　　　（noisy sound）
　　　　　　　かわいい　ねこ　　　（lovely cat）
　　　　　　　あたらしい　ほん　　（new book）
```
【→ Drill, Task 1, 2】

【GN❶-3】

この(this __), その(that __), あの(that __ over there) and どの(which __) are used only as modifiers of succeeding nouns. Compare these with これ(this one [near the speaker]), それ(that one [near the hearer]), あれ(that one [removed from both the speaker and the hearer]), どれ (which one). 　　　【→ Drill, Task 1, 2】

【GN❶-4】

Most of the sentences above are based on one of the following sentence patterns.

（1）

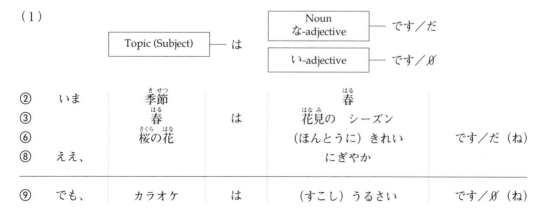

※Note that だ cannot be used with い-adjectives. 　　　　　　　　　　　　　　【→GN❶-1】

（2）

Location		に	Subject		が	あります／ある [inanimate] います／いる [animate]

④ ⑬	公園 （こうえん） 中国 （ちゅうごく）	に（も）	（大きい）桜の 木 （おお）（さくら）（き） お花見の しゅうかん （はなみ）	が	（たくさん）あります／ある あります（か）／ある
⑤			花見の 人 （はなみ）	が	（たくさん）います／いる

ここ(this place, here), そこ(that place, there), あそこ(that place over there, over there), and どこ(what place? where?) are often used as location words. It is usually the case that the topicalized noun moves to the front of the sentence. Therefore, when 木村さんたち(きむら) in the sentence どこに 木村さんたちが いますか(Where are Mr. Kimura and others?) becomes topicalized, it is most natural to say 木村さんたちは どこに いますか(As for Mr. Kimura and others, where are they?) as in Dialogue. When the subject-が becomes topicalized with は attached to it, が gets deleted, i.e. が + は = は. 【→ Task 1, 2】

DRILL

ドリル

例の ように、言いかえなさい。
（れい）　　　　（い）

Read the example, and paraphrase the following: 【→GN❶-1, 2, 3】

（例: example）

その おとは うるさい。 → それは うるさい おとだ。
その おとは うるさいです。 → それは うるさい おとです。
(That sound is noisy.) (That is a noisy sound.)

この へやは すてきだ。 → これは すてきな へやだ。
この へやは すてきです。 → これは すてきな へやです。
(This room is wonderful.) (This is a wonderful room.)

1　この 木は 大きい。 → （　　　　　　　　　　　）
　　（き）　（おお）
　　（　　　　　　　　　） → これは 大きい 木です。
　　(This tree is big.) (This is a big tree.)

2　（　　　　　　　　　） → それは きれいな 花だ。
　　　　　　　　　　　　　　　　　　　　　　　　（はな）
　　その 花は きれいです。 → （　　　　　　　　　　　）
　　(Those flowers are beautiful.) (Those are beautiful flowers.)

3　あの まちは にぎやかだ。 → （　　　　　　　　　　　）
　　（　　　　　　　　　） → あれは にぎやかな まちです。
　　(That town over there is bustling.) (That one over there is a bustling town.)

4　（　　　　　　　　　） → それは あたらしい ほんだ。
　　その ほんは あたらしいです。 → （　　　　　　　　　　　）
　　(That book is new.) (That is a new book.)

TASKS
タスク

(1) 絵さがし
Picture Search

【→GN❶-1, 2, 3, 4】

つぎの 会話1-4は a-dの どの
絵の 会話か かんがえて ください。

Find out which picture each dialogue refers to.

1　A：ここが ぼくの へやです。
　　　さあ、どうぞ。
　　B：すてきな へやですね。

2　B：あっ、ねこが いますね。
　　A：ええ、その ねこは
　　　ペルシャねこです。
　　B：かわいいですね。 なまえは？
　　A：タマです。 とても おもいですよ。

3　B：この ぼうしは とても
　　　きれいですね。
　　　がいこくの ぼうしですか。
　　A：ええ、それは アメリカの
　　　ともだちの プレゼントです。

4　B：本が たくさん ありますね。
　　　あれは ぜんぶ あなたのですか。
　　A：ええ。 あそこには あたらしい
　　　本も ふるい 本も あります。
　　　さあ、 コーヒーです。 どうぞ。

⬤ＶＯＣＡＢＵＬＡＲＹ

⬤ぼく = masculine 'I'⬤さあ、どうぞ = Oh, please [come in]⬤あっ = Oh!⬤ペルシャ = Persia, Persian⬤なまえ = name⬤おもい = heavy: い-adjective⬤ぼうし = hat, cap⬤がいこく = foreign country⬤アメリカ = America⬤ともだち = friend[s]⬤プレゼント = present, gift⬤ぜんぶ = all⬤あなたの = your, yours⬤ほん = book⬤ふるい = old: い-adjective⬤コーヒー = coffee

(2) ガンバ探偵の　事件メモ❶—犯人を　さがせ！

The Casebook of Detective Gamba ❶—Search for the Criminal!　　　　【→GN❶-1, 2, 3, 4】

ほうせきどろぼうの　犯人が　公園の　中に　います。

みんなで　さがしましょう。

The criminal, a jewelry thief, is in the park. Let's find him or her together.

ガンバ探偵の　メモ：

犯人は　わかい　男だ。

かみは　みじかい。　せは　たかい。

目は　ほそい。

犯人の　うしろに　いぬ　が　いる。

犯人は　でんわボックスの　そばに　いる。

その　でんわボックスは　公園の　中に　ある。

こんにちは。　わたしは
ガンバ探偵です。
どうぞ　よろしく！

⬤ V O C A B U L A R Y ⬤

●たんてい = detective ●じけん = case ●メモ = memo, book ●はんにん = criminal ●ほうせき = jewelry ●どろ ぼう = thief ●こんにちは = Hello! ●どうぞ　よろしく = how do you do, glad to know you ●わかい = young: い- adjective ●おとこ = male ●かみ = hair ●みじかい = short: い-adjective ●せ = height ●たかい = tall: い-adjective ●め = eye ●ほそい = narrow [eyes]: い-adjective ●うしろ = behind ●いぬ = dog ●でんわボックス = telephone booth ●なか = inside

❷ ゴールデンウィーク
Golden Week

This is a weeklong string of national holidays
in late April and early May.
Golden Week includes important commemorative days and festivals
like Midori no Hi (Greenery Day) on April 29,
Kenpo Kinenbi (Constitution Memorial Day) on May 3
and Kodomo no Hi (Children's Day) on May 5.
Not all Japanese stick around to observe them, however,
since Golden Week is a good chance
for office workers and students
to jet off to the sun in Saipan or Hawaii.
Other people prefer to relax at an *onsen* hot spring resort
or traditional country inn.
Either way, the airports and roads
are jam-packed during Golden Week.

MAIN TEXT — ほんぶん

Look at the picture on this page and read the following passage. Have you heard anything about Japan's "Golden Week" holidays?

ゴールデンウィーク

五月の　はじめに　ゴールデンウィークが　ある。　たくさんの
人が　ゴールデンウィークに　旅行を　する。　わたしの　友だちは
京都へ　行く。　わたしは　どこへも　行かない。

Golden Week
Golden Week comes at the beginning of May. During its consecutive holidays, many people take trips. My friend is going to Kyoto, but I'm not going anywhere.

Listen to and repeat after the tape. High and low pitches are marked with ⌐ and ⌐ , and the stressed word is in bold below.

Gogatsu-no hajime-ni **goorudenwiiku**-ga aru. Takusan-no hito-ga goorudenwiiku-ni **ryokoo**-o suru. Watashi-no tomodachi-wa **Kyooto**-e iku. Watashi-wa doko-e-mo **ikanai**.

EXPLANATION　せつめい

The following breakdown of terms will help you to understand the passage.

① ゴールデンウィーク

ゴールデンウィーク golden week: name given to consecutive holidays in the beginning of May

② 五月の　はじめに　ゴールデンウィークが　ある。

ごがつ May

の of: particle [= marker] to indicate the noun that modifies the succeeding noun

はじめ beginning

に on, in, at: here, particle to indicate time 【→GN❷-1】

が particle to indicate the subject, i.e., what is being talked about in the sentence

ある there is, there are, to have: the plain form of あります 【→GN❷-2】【→GN❶-1, 4 for existential sentences】

③ たくさんの　人が　ゴールデンウィークに　旅行を　する。

たくさん many, much

ひと person(s)

りょこう trip, traveling

を particle to indicate the [direct] object 【→GN❷-1】

する to do: the plain form of します [りょこうを　する means 'to travel'] 【→GN❷-2】

④ わたしの　友だちは　京都へ　行く。

わたしの my: わたし(I)＋の(of)

ともだち friend[s]

は as for, speaking of: particle to indicate the topic in the sentence 【→GN❶-4 for the topic particle は】

きょうと Kyoto: an ancient capital of Japan

へ to: direction particle. に may also be used for direction. 【→GN❷-1, Task 1】

いく to go: the plain form of いきます. [Since Japanese verbs (other than those in the past tense) typically indicate future (or habitual) actions, this sentence means 'My friend is going/will go to Kyoto.' 【→GN❷-1】

⑤ わたしは　どこへも　行かない。

どこ where

も also, too

いかない not to go: the plain form of いきません [An interrogative＋も with a negative often has all-exclusive meaning; i.e., どこへも　いかない means 'not to go anywhere.'] 【→GN❷-2, 3】

DIALOGUE — かいわ

Did you understand the passage? Look at the picture on the next page. In the following conversation Ms. Cooper and Mr. Kimura are talking about Golden Week.

クーパー：空が　きれいですね。

木村　　：ほんとに　気持ちが　いいですね。

クーパー：もうすぐ　ゴールデンウィークですね。

　　　　　　ゴールデンウィークの　プランは　ありますか。

木村　　：いいえ、何も　ありません。　クーパーさんは？

クーパー：わたしは　旅行を　します。

木村　　：そうですか。　うらやましいですね。　どこへ　行きますか。

クーパー：京都と　奈良へ　行きます。

Cooper: It's a nice clear day, isn't it?
Kimura: Makes you feel good, eh?
Cooper: It'll be Golden Week soon. Do you have any plans?
Kimura: No, none. What about you?
Cooper: I'm taking a trip.
Kimura: Really? I wish I could. Where are you going?
Cooper: To Kyoto and Nara.

PRONUNCIATION　はつおん

Listen to and repeat after the tape. Try to imitate well when practicing this exercise.

Cooper: Sora-ga **kiree**-desu-ne.

Kimura: **Hontoni** kimochi-ga ii-desu-ne.

Cooper: Moosugu **gooruden-wiiku**-desu-ne. Gooruden-wiiku-no puran-wa **arimasu**-ka.

Kimura: Iie, nani-mo **arimasen**. **Kuupaa**-san-wa?

Cooper: Watashi-wa **ryokoo**-o shimasu.

Kimura: Soo-desu-ka. **Urayamashii**-desu-ne. **Doko**-e ikimasu-ka.

Cooper: **Kyooto**-to **Nara**-e ikimasu.

| EXPLANATION | せつめい |

Did you understand the dialogue? If you didn't, the following explanation will help you to understand and enjoy it.

⑥空が　きれいですね。

そら sky

きれい clear, pretty: な-adjective 【→GN❶-1, 2 for adjectives】

です is, are: the polite form of the copula だ 【→GN ❶-1 for plain vs. polite forms】

ね isn't it true!: particle used at the end of a sentence for confirmation or exclamation

⑦ほんとに　気持ちが　いいですね。

ほんとに really, truly

きもち feeling, mood

いい good, well: い-adjective

⑧もうすぐ　ゴールデンウィークですね。

もうすぐ soon

⑨ゴールデンウィークの　プランは　ありますか。

プラン plan

あります to have, there is, there are: the polite form of ある

か particle to make a sentence into a question

⑩いいえ、何も　ありません。クーパーさんは？

いいえ no

なに what

ありません the negative form of あります[As in ⑤, an interogative＋も with a negative often has all-exclusive meaning; i.e., なにも　ありません means 'There are nothing/I have none.'] 【→GN❷-2, 3】

クーパーさんは？ How about you, Ms. Cooper?

⑪わたしは　旅行を　します。

わたし I

します to do: the polite form of する

⑫そうですか。うらやましいですね。どこへ　行きますか。

そうですか Is that right?

うらやましい enviable, envious: い-adjective

いきます to go: the polite form of いく

⑬京都と　奈良へ　行きます。

と and: particle to join only nouns

なら Nara: an ancient capital of Japan

GRAMMAR NOTES (GN❷)
ぶんぽうノート

【GN❷-1】

The new sentence pattern introduced in this unit is found in verb-based constructions like the following. に, を, and へ indicate nouns relating to time, the direct object, and a direction respectively. Note that に can also indicate a direction noun.

【→Drill 1, Task 1】

SUBJECT/TOPIC - が／は	(…に／を／へ, etc.)	VERB
③たくさんの 人が	ゴールデンウィークに　　　旅行を	する。
⑪わたしは	旅行を	します。
④わたしの 友だちは	京都へ	行く。
⑤わたしは	どこへも	行かない。
⑫	どこへ	行きますか。
⑬	京都と 奈良へ	行きます。

【GN❷-2】

As shown below, Japanese verbs can be divided into -ru ending verbs and -u ending verbs, and different verb forms can be derived by changing -(r)u to -(a)nai (plain, negative), -(i)masu (polite, affirmative), and -(i)masen (polite, negative). The polite forms should be used when you are expected to be polite to the listener or the reader. Otherwise, the plain forms (the affirmative forms of which appear in the dictionary) may be used. These verbs, all of them in tenses other than the past, usually refer to future or habitual actions.　【→Drill 1, 2, Task 1】

	plain form		polite form	
	affirmative(-ru)	negative(-nai)	affirmative(-masu)	negative(-masen)
-ru ending verb	たべる(tabe-ru)	たべない(tabe-nai)	たべます(tabe-masu)	たべません(tabe-masen)
	ねる(ne-ru)	ねない(ne-nai)	ねます(ne-masu)	ねません(ne-masen)
	みる(mi-ru)	みない(mi-nai)	みます(mi-masu)	みません(mi-masen)
	affirmative(-u)	negative(-anai)	affirmative(-imasu)	negative(-imasen)
-u ending verb	いく(ik-u)	いかない(ik-anai)	いきます(ik-imasu)	いきません(ik-imasen)
	のむ(nom-u)	のまない(nom-anai)	のみます(nom-imasu)	のみません(nom-imasen)
	すう(su[w]-u)	すわない(suw-anai)	すいます(su[w]-imasu)	すいません(su[w]-imasen)

●たべる = to eat ●ねる = to sleep, go to bed ●みる = to watch, look ●のむ = to drink ●すう = to smoke, inhale

※In modern Japanese, [wu] and [wi] are pronounced [u] and [i] respectively.
※There are two verbs which inflect irregularly; 'to do'（する, しない, します, しません）and 'to come'（くる, こない, きます, きません）, which you simply have to memorize. Note also that the negative of ある is ない;（ある, ない, あります, ありません）　　　【→Task 2】

【GN❷-3】

As mentioned in the explanation of terms, an interrogative＋も with a negative often has all-exclusive meaning. Review sentences ⑤ and ⑩.　　　【→Drill 2, Task 1】

だれ(who)	→だれも	+negative (nobody...)
なに(what)	→なにも	+negative (nothing....)
どこへ([to] where)	→どこへも	+negative ([to] nowhere....)

DRILLS
ドリル

（1）あなたは　Aと　Bの　どちらですか。

Which applies to you, A or B?　　　　　　　　　　　　　　　　【→GN❷-1, 2】

わたしは　　　　　　　　　A　　　　　　　　　　B

1　まいにち　日本語を　　　[はなします(←はなす)　・はなしません(←はなさない)]
2　ぎんこうから　お金を　　[かります(←かりる)　・かりません（←かりない)]
3　よく　公園で　　　　　　[あそびます(←あそぶ)　・あそびません(←あそばない)]
4　まいあさ　まどを　　　　[あけます(←あける)　・あけません(←あけない)]
5　あした　プールで　　　　[およぎます(←およぐ)　・およぎません(←およがない)]
6　きょう　てがみを　　　　[かきます(←かく)　・かきません(←かかない)]

（2）例に　ならって、こたえなさい。

Give the answer as shown in the example.　　　　　　　　　　【→GN❷-2, 3】

例　だれが　いますか。　　→　　だれも　いません。
　　(Who's there?)　　　　　　　(Nobody's there.)
1　だれが　きますか。　　→　　＿＿＿＿＿＿＿＿＿＿
　　(Who's coming?)　　　　　　 (Nobody's coming.)
2　何が　ありますか。　　→　　＿＿＿＿＿＿＿＿＿＿
　　(What's there?)　　　　　　　(Nothing's there.)
3　何を　たべますか。　　→　　＿＿＿＿＿＿＿＿＿＿
　　(What are you going to eat?)　(I'm not going to eat anything.)
4　どこへ　行きますか。　→　　＿＿＿＿＿＿＿＿＿＿
　　(Where are you going?)　　　(I'm not going anyhere.)

VOCABULARY

1

●あなた = you ●どちら = which of the two ●まいにち = every day ●にほんご = Japanese language ●はなす = to speak ●ぎんこうから = from the bank: ぎんこう[bank] + から[from] ●おかね = money ●かりる = to borrow ●よく = often ●こうえん = park ●あそぶ = to play ●まいあさ = every morning ●まど = window ●あける = to open ●あした = tomorrow ●プール = swimming pool ●およぐ = to swim ●きょう = today ●てがみ = letter ●かく = to write

TASKS
タスク

(1) レジャースポットを 探そう

Let's search for the leisure spots.

【→GN❷-1, 2, 3】

ゴールデンウィークの　プランは　ありますか。　日本の　すてきな
レジャースポットを　しょうかいします。　「はい」（ ➡ ）と
「いいえ」（ ⟶ ）で　こたえて　ください。

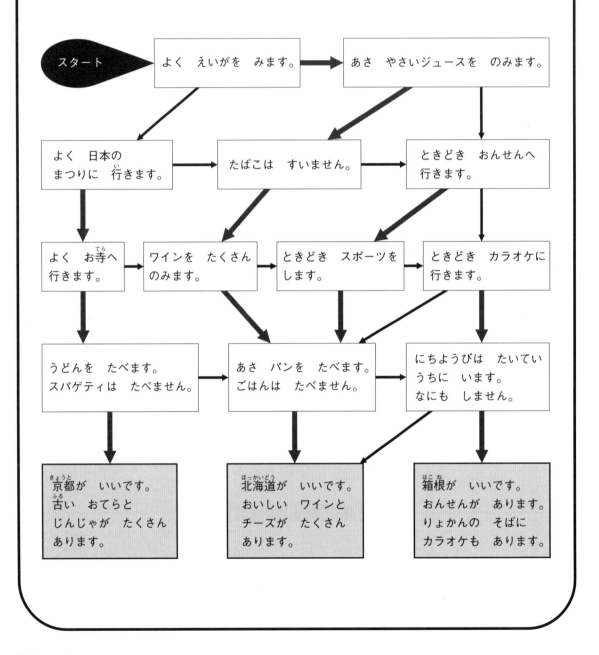

| スタート | よく　えいがを　みます。 | あさ　やさいジュースを　のみます。 |

| よく　日本の　まつりに　行きます。 | たばこは　すいません。 | ときどき　おんせんへ　行きます。 |

| よく　お寺へ　行きます。 | ワインを　たくさん　のみます。 | ときどき　スポーツを　します。 | ときどき　カラオケに　行きます。 |

| うどんを　たべます。スパゲティは　たべません。 | あさ　パンを　たべます。ごはんは　たべません。 | にちようびは　たいてい　うちに　います。なにも　しません。 |

京都が　いいです。
古い　おてらと
じんじゃが　たくさん
あります。

北海道が　いいです。
おいしい　ワインと
チーズが　たくさん
あります。

箱根が　いいです。
おんせんが　あります。
りょかんの　そばに
カラオケも　あります。

(2) ガンバ探偵の　事件メモ❷—なぞなぞ

The Casebook of Detective Gamba ❷—Enigma 　　　　　　　　【→GN❷-2, GN❶-4】

ガンバ探偵の　つくえの　上に　へんな　てがみが　あります。　大どろぼうの
ＫＧ博士からの　手紙です。　これは　なぞなぞです。　さて、答えは　なんでしょう。

There is a peculiar letter on Detective Gamba's desk. The letter is from Dr. K.G., a notorious thief. This is an enigma. Now, what will be the answer?

1 「りんご」に　ある。　しかし、「ぶどう」には　ない。
2 「きりん」に　ある。　しかし、「いぬ」には　ない。
3 「げんかん」に　ある。　しかし、「だいどころ」には　ない。
4 「てんごく」に　ある。　しかし、「じごく」には　ない。
5 「しけん」に　ある。　しかし、「テスト」には　ない。

　　　　　　　　　　　　　　　　　　　　　答え＿＿＿＿＿＿＿

VOCABULARY

1

●レジャースポット = leisure spot●さがそう = let's search●にほん = Japan●すてきな = wonderful: な-adjective●しょうかいします = to introduce: the polite form of しょうかいする●で = with: here, instrumental particle●こたえて ください = please answer: the polite request form of こたえる[to answer]●スタート = start●えいが = movie●あさ = [in the] morning●やさい = vegetable●ジュース = juice●まつり = festival●たばこ = cigarette, tobacco●ときどき = sometimes●おんせん = hot spring [resort]●おてら = temple●ワイン = wine●スポーツ = sports●カラオケ = karaoke music●うどん = noodles●スパゲティ = spaghetti●パン = bread●ごはん = steamed rice●にちようび = Sunday●たいてい = usually●うちに = at home: うち[home]+に[at]●います = to be, to stay: the polite form of いる●いい = good: い-adjective●ふるい = old: い-adjective●じんじゃ = Shinto shrine●ほっかいどう = Hokkaido [a northern island in Japan]●おいしい = delicious: い-adjective●チーズ = cheese●はこね = Hakone [a hot spring resort near Tokyo]●りょかん = Japanese-style inn●そば = next to

2

●たんてい = detective●じけん = case●メモ = memo, book●なぞなぞ = puzzle, enigma●つくえ = desk●うえ = on●へんな = strange, peculiar: な - adjective●おおどろぼう = notorious thief: おお[big] + どろぼう[thief]●はかせ = Dr.●これ = this [one]●さて = well, now●こたえ = answer●なん = what=なに●でしょう = will probably be: uncertain version of です●りんご = apple●しかし = but, however: conjunction●ぶどう = grape●きりん = giraffe●いぬ = dog●げんかん = entrance●だいどころ = kitchen●てんごく = heaven●じごく = hell●しけん = test, examination●テスト = test

③ 結婚式
Wedding

Take a look at the mass of wedding-related advertisements
on subway trains for an idea of the time
and money Japanese spend on that special day.
Weddings today are often a mish-mash
of ancient and modern, Japanese and Western.
For instance, the couple may first perform a ritual Shinto exchange of
sake in traditional clothes–white kimono and
tsunokakushi headdress for the bride
and baggy *hakama* trousers and kimono for the groom–before
donning the flouncy white dress and snappy suit
of a typical Western wedding for the lavish reception,
which usually takes place in a hotel, restaurant or special wedding hall.
Many couples also take Christian vows of
marriage regardless of their religion.

MAIN TEXT — ほんぶん

Read the following passage. Have you ever been to a Japanese wedding ceremony and/or reception?

結婚式
けっこんしき

きのう　結婚式へ　行った。　ジューンブライドは　友だちの
　　　けっこんしき　　い　　　　　　　　　　　　　　　　とも
伊藤さんだ。　すてきな　ウェディングドレスだった。　ひろうえんの
いとう
ごちそうも　おいしかった。

Wedding
I went to a wedding yesterday. The June bride was my friend, Ms. Ito. Her wedding dress was beautiful and the reception feast was delicious.

PRONUNCIATION　はつおん

Listen to and repeat after the tape. High-and-low pitches are marked with ⌐ and ¬ and the stressed word is in bold below.

Kinoo **kekkonshiki**-e itta. Juunburaido-wa tomodachi-no **Itoo**-san-da. Sutekina **uedingudoresu**-datta. Hirooen-no gochisoo-mo **oishikatta**.

EXPLANATION　せつめい

The following breakdown of terms will help you to understand the passage.

①結婚式

けっこんしき wedding ceremony

②きのう　結婚式へ　行った。

きのう yesterday

へ to: direction particle 【→GN❷-1 for related particles】

いった went: the past tense of いく 【→GN❸-1】

③ジューンブライドは　友だちの 伊藤さんだ。

ジューンブライド June bride

は as for, speaking of: particle to indicate the topic in the sentence 【→GN❶-4 for the topic particle は】

ともだち friend

の of: particle to indicate the noun that modifies a succeeding noun

いとうさん Ms. Ito

だ is, are: copula 【→ GN❶-1, 4 for copulas】

④すてきな　ウェディングドレスだった。

すてきな wonderful: な-adjective 【→GN❶-2 for な-adjective】

ウェディングドレス wedding dress

だった was, were: the past tense of だ 【→GN❸-1】

⑤ひろうえんの　ごちそうも　おいしかった。

ひろうえん reception

ごちそう meal, feast

も also, too

おいしかった was delicious: the past tense of おいしい 【→GN❸-1】

DIALOGUE — かいわ

Did you understand the passage? If not, look at the picture again. In the following conversation, Ms. Chen is talking to Mr. Kaneda about a wedding ceremony she attended.

陳　：きのう　結婚式へ　行きました。

金田：ああ、あの　伊藤さんの　結婚式ですね。

陳　：そうです。　ウェディングドレスの　伊藤さん、すてきでしたよ。

金田：そうですか。　ひろうえんは　どうでしたか。

陳　：スピーチは　つまらなかったですが、ごちそうは　とても

　　　おいしかったです。

Chen: I went to a wedding yesterday.
Kaneda: Oh yes, your friend Ms. Ito's, right?
Chen: Yes. She looked gorgeous in her wedding dress.
Kaneda: Really? How was the reception?
Chen: The speeches were boring, but the food was excellent.

Listen to and repeat after the tape. Try to imitate well when practicing this exercise.

Chen: Kinoo **kekkonshiki**-e ikimashita.

Kaneda: Aa, ano **Itoo**-san-no kekkonshiki-desu-ne.

Chen: **Soo**-desu. Uedingudoresu-no Itoo-san, **suteki**-deshita-yo.

Kaneda: **Soo**-desu-ka. **Hirooen**-wa doo-deshita-ka.

Chen: Supiichi-wa tsumaranakatta-desu-ga, gochisoo-wa totemo **oishikatta**-desu.

EXPLANATION　せつめい

Did you understand the dialogue? If you didn't, the following explanation will help you to understand and enjoy it.

⑥きのう　結婚式へ　**行きました**。

いきました went: the polite form of いった 【→GN
❸-1】

⑦ああ、あの　伊藤さんの
結婚式ですね。

ああ Ah! Oh!
あの that __ : This あの refers to knowledge shared by
the speaker and the listener 【→GN❶-3 for
demonstratives】
です is, are: the polite form of だ here 【→GN❶-1, 4
for plain vs. polite forms】
ね isn't it?: particle used at the end of a sentence for
confirmation

⑧そうです。ウェディングドレスの
伊藤さん、すてきでしたよ。

そうです That's right.
でした was: the past tense of です 【→GN❸- 1】
よ you know: particle used at the end of a sentence for
emphasis

⑨そうですか。ひろうえんは
どうでしたか。

そうですか Is that right?
どう how
か particle to make a sentence into a question

⑩スピーチは　つまらなかったですが、
ごちそうは　とても
おいしかったです。

スピーチ speech
つまらなかったです were boring: the polite form of
つまらなかった [Note that つまらなかっただ is
ungrammatical.] 【→GN❸-1】
が but: this が, when attached to a sentence, connects
two sentences which are usually in contrast. 【→
GN❸-2】
とても very
おいしかったです was delicious: the polite form of
おいしかった 【→GN❸-1】

GRAMMAR NOTES (GN❸)
ぶんぽうノート

【GN❸-1】

Deriving past tenses. As shown below, the past tenses of Japanese predicates can be derived by changing the predicate endings accordingly.

【→ Drill 1, 2, Task 1, 2】

Plain Form

		affirmative		negative	
Noun or な -adj.	non-past	ごちそうだ すてきだ	[-da]	ごちそうでは　ない すてきでは　ない	[-dewa nai]
	past	ごちそうだった すてきだった	[-datta]	ごちそうでは　なかった すてきでは　なかった	[-dewa nakatta]
い -adj.	non-past	おいしい	[-i]	おいしく　ない	[-ku nai]
	past	おいしかった	[-katta]	おいしく　なかった	[-ku nakatta]
-ru verb	non-past	たべる	[-ru]	たべない	[-nai]
	past	たべた	[-ta]	たべなかった	[-nakatta]
-u verb	non-past	はなす	[-(s)u]	はなさない	[-(s)anai]
	past	はなした	[-(shi)ta] (＊)	はなさなかった	[-(s)anakatta]

＊ The past, affirmative plain form of -u ending verbs varies according to the stem of the verb as in the next page.

Polite form

		affirmative		negative	
Noun or な -adj.	non-past	ごちそうです すてきです	[-desu]	ごちそうでは　ありません すてきでは　ありません	[-dewa arimasen]
	past	ごちそうでした すてきでした	[-deshita]	ごちそうでは　ありませんでした すてきでは　ありませんでした [-dewa arimasendeshita]	
い -adj.	non-past	おいしいです	[-idesu]	おいしく　ないです　[-ku naidesu] おいしく ありません　[-ku arimasen]	
	past	おいしかったです [-kattadesu]		おいしく　なかったです　[-ku nakattadesu] おいしく ありませんでした [-ku arimasendeshita]	
-ru verb	non-past	たべます	[-masu]	たべません	[-masen]
	past	たべました	[-mashita]	たべませんでした	[-masendeshita]
-u verb	non-past	はなします	[-(sh)imasu]	はなしません	[-(sh)imasen]
	past	はなしました	[-(sh)imashita]	はなしませんでした	[-(sh)imasendeshita]

● たべる to eat ● はなす = to speak, to talk

(to write) かく→かいた (to listen) きく→きいた 　　　　　[-ku]　[-ita]	(to swim)　およぐ→およいだ (to hurry)　いそぐ→いそいだ 　　　　　　[-gu]　[-ida]	(to talk)　はなす→はなした (to drop)　おとす→おとした 　　　　　[-su]　　[-shita]
(to wait)　まつ→まった (to stand)　たつ→たった 　　　　　[-tsu]　[-tta]	(to die)　しぬ→しんだ 　　　　　　[-nu]　[-nda]	(to play)　　あそぶ→あそんだ (to fly, jump)　とぶ　→とんだ 　　　　　　　[-bu]　　　[-nda]
(to read)　よむ　→よんだ (to steal)　ぬすむ→ぬすんだ 　　　　　[-mu]　　[-nda]	(to sell)　うる→うった (to ride)　のる→のった 　　　　　　[-ru]　[-tta]	(to buy)　かう　→かった (to sing)　うたう→うたった 　　　　　[-(w)u]　　[-tta]

※ Note that the inflection of いく (to go)→いった is somewhat unusual. Note also that the negative ない inflects just like い-adjective.

※ The irregular verbs する (to do) and くる (to come), mentioned also in 【GN❷-2】, inflect as follows:

	Plain Form		Polite Form	
	affirmative	negative	affirmative	negative
non-past past	する した	しない しなかった	します しました	しません しませんでした
non-past past	くる きた	こない こなかった	きます きました	きません きませんでした

【GN❸-2】

The particle が, when attached to a sentence, connects two sentences which are usually, but not necessarily, in contrast. (Remember that が attached to a noun indicates the subject of a sentence.) 【→GN❶-4】【→Drill 2】

（1）陳さんは　結婚式へ　行ったが、わたしは　行かなかった。
　　　Ms. Chen went to a wedding ceremony, but I didn't.

（2）ひろうえんの　スピーチは　つまらなかったですが、ごちそうは　おいしかったです。
　　　The speeches during the reception were boring, but the feast was delicious.

（3）日本には　花見の　しゅうかんが　ありますが、中国にも　ありますか。
　　　There is a flower-viewing custom in Japan, [but] is there one in China, too?

（4）せんしゅうは　ゴールデンウィークでしたが、何を　しましたか。
　　　Last week was golden week, [but] what did you do?

DRILLS

ドリル

（１）クーパーさんの　日記を　かんせいさせなさい。

Complete Ms. Cooper's diary, using the verbs below.　　　　　　　　　　【→GN❸-1】

クーパーさんの　日記
ゴールデンウィークに　京都へ（1　　　　　　　）。　まつりを（2　　　　　　　）。
人が　たくさん（3　　　　　　　）が、とても（4　　　　　　　）。　まいにち
日本語を（5　　　　　　　）。アメリカの　かぞくへ　はがきを（6　　　　　　　）。

〔　話した　　行った　　書いた　　おもしろかった　　いた　　見た　〕

（２）文を　かんせいさせなさい。

Complete each sentence by connecting 1-4 with a-d.　　　　　　　　　　【→GN❸-1, 2】

1　ひろうえんの　ごちそうは　おいしかったですが、

2　桜の　花は　きれいでしたが、

3　友だちは　京都へ　行きましたが、

4　たばこは　すいませんが、

a　お酒は　のみます。

b　わたしは　どこへも　行きませんでした。

c　スピーチは　つまらなかったです。

d　カラオケは　うるさかったです。

VOCABULARY

1
●クーパーさん = Ms. Cooper ●にっき = diary ●かんせいさせなさい= complete: an imperative form of かんせいさせる[to complete] ●に = here, particle to indicate time ●きょうと = Kyoto: an ancient capital of Japan ●まつり = festival ●ひと = person ●が = here, particle to indicate the subject of a sentence ●たくさん = many, much ●まいにち = every day ●にほんご = Japanese language: にほん[Japan]+ご[language] ●アメリカ = America ●かぞく = family ●はがき = post card ●おもしろかった = was interesting: the past tense of おもしろい[interesting] ●いた = there was / were: the past tense of いる[to exist] ●みた = watched: the past tene of みる[to watch, to look]

2
●ぶん = sentence ●おさけ = お[a polite preifx]+さけ[Japanese sake, or any alcoholic beverage] ●さくらの　はな = cherry blossoms ●きれい = pretty, attractive: な-adjective ●どこへも +negative= [to] nowhere【→GN❷-3 for related expressions】 ●たばこ = cigarette, tobacco ●すいます = to smoke, to inhale: the polite form of すう[to smoke: to inhale] ●カラオケ = karaoke music ●うるさかった = was noisy: the past tense of うるさい [noisy]

TASKS
タスク

(1) 新婚旅行の　思い出

Honeymoon Memories

【→GN❸-1】

伊藤さんたちは　北海道へ　新婚旅行に　行きました。新婚旅行の　アルバムを
作ります。　下の　写真には　A～Dの　どの　ラベルが　いいですか。

《写真》

1 (　　　　)

2 (　　　　)

3 (　　　　)

4 (　　　　)

《ラベル》

A　6月1日
牧場で　馬に
乗った。　すこし
こわかった。

B　6月2日
グランドホテルに
泊まった。　大きい
ホテルだった。
温泉も　あった。

C　6月3日
有名な　時計台を
見た。　観光客が
たくさん　いた。

D　6月4日
空港で　バターや
チーズや　肉など
おみやげを
たくさん　買った。

(2) ガンバ探偵の　事件メモ ❸ ―うそは　どれだ？

The Casebook of Detective Gamba ❸—Which is Untrue? 　　　　　【→GN❸-1】

どろぼうＸは　いろいろな　ことを　言いました。　しかし、うそが　あります。
その　うそを　さがして　ください。

どろぼうＸ

7:00 a.m.　　起きた　………A

8:30
　　　　会社へ　行った　………B

9:00
　　　　仕事を　した　…………C

12:00
　　　　昼ごはんを　食べた　…D

1:00 p.m.
　　　　仕事を　した　…………E

5:00

5:30
　　　　プールで　およいだ　…F

7:30
　　　　バーで　酒を　飲んだ　G

10:00
　　　　家へ　かえった　………H

10:30

しょうにん

●アパートの　となりの　人
「Ｘさんは　10時ごろ　かえりました。　わたしと
同じ　電車で　かえりました。」

●バーの　ママ
「Ｘさんは　7時半に　来ました。ビールを
のみました。　2時間半ぐらい　いました。

●スイミングクラブの　友だち
「Ｘさんは　5時半ごろ　来ました。　30分ぐらい
いました。」

●どろぼうＸの　会社の　人
「会社は　9時から　5時までです。」

VOCABULARY

1

● しんこんりょこう = honeymoon: しんこん[newlyweds]+りょこう[trip] ● おもいで = memory, reminiscence ● いとうさんたち = the Itos ● ほっかいどう = Hokkaido [a northern Island of Japan ● に = particle indicating a purpose [(しんこんりょこう)に] or goal [(うま)に][(ホテル)に] ● アルバム = album ● つくります = to make: the polite form of つくる[to make] ● したの = below ● しゃしん = photo ● どの = which __ ● ラベル = label ● いい = good: い-adjective ● ろくがつ = June ● ついたち = the first day of the month ● ぼくじょう = ranch ● で = particle indicating the location where an action takes place ● うま = horse ● すこし = a little ● こわかった = was scary: the past tense of こわい[scary] ● ふつか = the second day of the month ● グランドホテル = Grand Hotel ● とまった = stayed: the past tense of とまる[to stay] ● おんせん = hot spring [resort] ● あった = there was: the past tense of ある[to exist] ● みっか = the third day of the month ● ゆうめいな = famous: な-adjective ● とけいだい = clock tower ● かんこうきゃく = tourists ● よっか = the fourth day of the month ● くうこう = airport ● バター = butter ● チーズ = cheese ● にく = meat ● ～や～など = and other things ● おみやげ = souvenir

2

● たんてい = detective ● じけん = case ● メモ = memo, book ● うそ = lie ● どれ = which [one] ● どろぼう = thief ● いろいろな = various: な-adjective ● こと = things ● いいました = said: the past tense of いいます[to say] ● しかし = but ● あります = to exist: the polite form of ある[to exist] ● その = that __ ● さがして ください = please find: the polite request form of さがす[to look for] ● おきた = got up: the past tense of おきる[to get up] ● かいしゃ = company ● しごと = work, job ● ひるごはん = lunch ● プール = swimming pool ● バー = bar ● うち = home ● かえった = returned [home]: the past tense of かえる[to return home] ● しょうにん = witness ● アパート = apartment ● となり = neighbor ● じゅうじ = ten o'clock ● ごろ = around, about: an approximate point in time ● かえりました = returned [home]: the past tense of かえります[to return home] ● ～と おなじ = the same as... ● でんしゃ = train ● で = by: here, an instrumental particle ● ママ = manager, proprietress: a woman who manages a bar is often called ママ ● しちじはんに = at seven-thirty: しち[seven]+じ[o'clock]+はん[a half]+に[at] ● ビール = beer ● にじかん = for two hours: に[two]+じかん[hour] ● ぐらい = about: approximate duration of time ● いました = stayed: the past tense of います[to exist, to stay] ● スイミングクラブ = swimming club ● ご = five ● さんじゅっぷん = thirty minutes ● く = nine ● から = from ● まで = until

④ たなばた
Tanabata

One of five prominant festivals,
Tanabata is usually held on July 7
to celebrate the once-a-year lover's reunion
between the weaver maiden star
and the cowherd star.
During Tanabata,
whose legend is based on
both Chinese and Japanese folklore,
houses are decorated with bamboo branches
and various talismen.
Another customary feature is long,
thin strips of paper called *tanzaku*,
on which people
write wishes and sometimes poems.

MAIN TEXT — ほんぶん

Look at the picture below and read the following passage about Tanabata (the Star Festival) in Japan. Have you heard of this festival?

たなばた

クーパーさんは　木村さんの　うちで　たなばたを　祝った。　竹の
えだに　いろいろな　ものが　かざって　あった。　木村さんの
おくさんは　きれいな　ゆかたを　着て　いた。　クーパーさんは
アメリカの　まつりを　思いだして　いた。

Tanabata
Ms. Cooper celebrated Tanabata at Mr. Kimura's house. Bamboo branches were decorated with various things. Mr. Kimura's wife was wearing a pretty summer kimono. Ms. Cooper recalled festivals in the United States.

Listen to and repeat after the tape. High and low pitches are marked with ⌐ and ¬, and the stressed word is in bold below.

Kuupaa-san-wa Kimura-san-no uchi-de **Tanabata**-o iwatta. Take-no eda-ni iroirona mono-ga **kazatte** atta. Kimura-san-no okusan-wa kireena **yukata**-o kite ita. Kuupaa-san-wa **America**-no matsuri-o omoidashite ita.

EXPLANATION　せつめい

The following breakdown of terms will help you to understand the passage.

① たなばた

たなばた the Star Festival [from China, this July seventh festival celebrates the Herdsman and the Weaver on opposite sides of the Milky Way, who are symbolized as lovers.]

② クーパーさんは　木村さんの　うちで　たなばたを　祝った。

クーパーさん Ms. Cooper

は as for, speaking of: particle [marker] to indicate the topic in the sentence 【→GN❶-4 for the topic particle は】

きむらさん Mr. Kimura

の of: particle to indicate a noun that modifies a succeeding noun

うち house, home

で at, in, on: particle to indicate a location where an action takes place

を particle to indicate the [direct] object of the verb 【→GN❷-1 for related particles】

いわった the past tense of いわう[to celebrate] 【→GN❸-1 for the past tenses】

③ 竹の　えだに　いろいろな　ものが　かざって　あった。

たけ bamboo
えだ branch
に on, at, in, to: a location particle [here, used to indicate

the goal of an action]

いろいろな various: な-adjective 【→GN❶-2 for な-adjective】

もの thing[s]

が particle to indicate the subject, i.e., what is being talked about in the sentence 【→GN❶-4 for the particle が】

かざって the て-form of かざる [to decorate] 【→GN❹-1, 2】

あった the past tense of ある[to exist], used here as part of a ～て ある expression 【→GN❹-2】

④ 木村さんの　おくさんは　きれいな　ゆかたを　着て　いた。

おくさん [someone's] wife; [my] wife is かない or つま
きれいな pretty, attractive: な-adjective
ゆかた informal summer kimono
きて the て-form of きる[to wear] 【→GN❹-1】
いた the past tense of いる[to exist], used here as part of ～て いる expression 【→GN❹-1】

⑤ クーパーさんは　アメリカの　まつりを　思いだして　いた。

アメリカ America
まつり festival
おもいだして the て-form of おもいだす [to recall, to remember] 【→GN❹-1】

DIALOGUE かいわ

Did you understand the passage? Following is the conversation between Ms. Cooper and Mr. Kimura on the day of the Star Festival.

クーパー：木村さん、この　かざりは　何ですか。　日本語が　書いて

　　　　　ありますね。

木村　　：ああ、それは　たんざくです。　たんざくには　しや

　　　　　ねがいごとが　書いて　あります。

クーパー：そうですか。　あそこで　子どもたちが　何か　して

　　　　　いますが、あれは　何ですか。

木村　　：あれは　きんぎょすくいです。　きんぎょは　小さい

　　　　　さかなです。　おもしろいですよ。

クーパー：そうですか。　でも、きんぎょが　少し　かわいそうですね。

Cooper: Mr. Kimura, what's this decoration? It's got something written on it in Japanese.
Kimura: Oh, that's *tanzaku*; it has poems and wishes written on it.
Cooper: Oh, really? And what are the children doing over there?
Kimura: They're scooping up tiny goldfish. It's a lot of fun, you know.
Cooper: Is it? I feel a bit sorry for the goldfish.

PRONUNCIATION はつおん

Listen to and repeat after the tape. Try to imitate well when practicing this exercise.

Cooper: Kimura-san, kono kazari-wa **nan**-desu-ka. **Nihongo**-ga kaite-arimasu-ne.
Kimura: Aa, sore-wa **tanzaku**-desu. Tanzaku-ni-wa **shi**-ya **negaigoto**-ga kaite-arimasu.
Cooper: **Soo**-desu-ka. Asoko-de kodomotachi-ga nanika shite-imasu-ga, are-wa **nan**-desu-ka.
Kimura: Are-wa **kingyosukui**-desu. Kingyo-wa chiisai **sakana**-desu. **Omoshiroi**-desu-yo.
Cooper: **Soo**-desu-ka. Demo, kingyo-ga sukoshi **kawaisoo**-desu-ne.

Did you understand the dialogue? If you didn't, the following breakdown of terms will help you to understand and enjoy it.

⑥木村さん、この　かざりは
　何ですか。

この this ＿【→GN❶-3 for similar demonstratives】
かざり decoration
なん what
です is, are: the polite form of the copula だ【→GN❶-1, 4 for copulas】
か particle to make a sentence into a question

⑦日本語が　書いて　ありますね。

にほんご the Japanese language
かいて the て-form of かく[to write]
あります the polite form of ある[to exist]【→GN❹-2】
ね Isn't it true!: particle used at the end of a sentence for confirmation or exclamation

⑧ああ、それは　たんざくです。

ああ Ah!, Oh!
それ that one [near the listener]: demonstrative【→GN❶-3 for demonstratives】

⑨たんざくには　しや　ねがいごとが
　書いて　あります。

たんざく a strip of paper for poems, etc.
し poem
や and [so on]
ねがいごと wish[es]

⑩そうですか。あそこで
　子どもたちが　何か　して
　いますが、あれは　何ですか。

そうですか Is that right?
あそこ that place [over there]【→GN❶-4 for similar location words】
こどもたち children: こども[child]+たち[plural suffix]
なにか something
して the て-form of する[to do]
います the polite form of いる[to exist]【→GN❹-1】
が but: conjunction【→GN❸-2 for the conjunction が】
あれ that one [over there]: demonstrative

⑪あれは　きんぎょすくいです。
　きんぎょは　小さい　さかなです。

きんぎょすくい scooping for goldfish: きんぎょ[goldfish]+すくい[scooping]
ちいさい small: い-adjective【→GN❶-2 for い-adjective】
さかな fish

⑫おもしろいですよ。

おもしろい fun, interesting: い-adjective
よ particle used at the end of a sentence for emphasis

⑬そうですか。　でも、きんぎょが
　少し　かわいそうですね。

でも but: conjunction, more informal than しかし
すこし a little
かわいそう pitiful, unfortunate: な-adjective【→GN❶-2 for な-adjective】

GRAMMAR NOTES (GN❹)
ぶんぽうノート

【GN❹-1】

〈Verb-て／で＋いる〉 The verb-て／で＋いる indicates either an action in progress, as in (1), or a state of being, as in (2), depending on the verb.

（1） こどもたちが きんぎょすくいを して いる。
The children are goldfish-scooping.

（2） あの ひとは しんで いる。
That person is dead [NOT "That person is dying."]

Refer also to sentences ④, ⑤, and ⑩ in the Main Text and the Dialogue.

④木村さんの おくさんは きれいな ゆかたを 着て いた。
⑤クーパーさんは アメリカの まつりを 思いだして いた。
⑩あそこで 子どもたちが 何か して いますが、あれは 何ですか。

The verb-て／で form can be derived by changing た／だ portion of the plain past form into て／で. (Please review 【GN❸-1】 for the plain past forms.)

(to eat)	たべる	→ たべた	→ たべて	(to wear)	きる	→ きた	→ きて
(to write)	かく	→ かいた	→ かいて	(to swim)	およぐ	→ およいだ	→ およいで
(to talk)	はなす	→ はなした	→ はなして	(to wait)	まつ	→ まった	→ まって
(to die)	しぬ	→ しんだ	→ しんで	(to play)	あそぶ	→ あそんだ	→ あそんで
(to read)	よむ	→ よんだ	→ よんで	(to sell)	うる	→ うった	→ うって
(to buy)	かう	→ かった	→ かって	(to go)	いく	→ いった	→ いって
(to do)	する	→ した	→ して	(to come)	くる	→ きた	→ きて

【→ Drill, Task 2】

【GN❹-2】

〈Transitive Verb-て／で＋ある〉 The transitive verb-て／で＋ある indicates a state of being that has resulted from an action. Therefore, sentence (3) with the transitive verb あける→あけて implies that someone opened the window. There is no such implication in the intransitive verb あく→あいて in sentence (4). Transitive verbs are those that take [direct] objects marked with を, e.g., まどを あける (to open the window).【→GN❷-1 for the particle を】

（3） まどが あけて ある。The window is opened [by someone].
（4） まどが あいて いる。The window is open.

Refer also to sentences ③, ⑦, and ⑨ in the Main Text and the Dialogue.

③竹の えだに いろいろな ものが かざって あった。
⑦日本語が 書いて ありますね。
⑨たんざくには しや ねがいごとが 書いて あります。

【→ Task 1】

DRILL
ドリル

38ページの　絵を　見て　文を　かんせいさせなさい。

Look at the picture on p.38, and complete the sentences. Using the verbs below. 【→GN❹-1】

例：たくさんの　人が　たなばたを　祝っています。（←祝う）
　　　(Many people are celebrating the Star Festival.)

1　子どもたちが　きんぎょすくいを　＿＿＿＿＿＿＿＿＿。

2　木村さんと　クーパーさんは　ビールを　＿＿＿＿＿＿＿＿＿。

3　木村さんの　おくさんは　ゆかたを　＿＿＿＿＿＿＿＿＿。

4　屋台で　わたがしや　りんごあめを　＿＿＿＿＿＿＿＿＿。

5　小さい　子どもが　大きい　ぬいぐるみを　＿＿＿＿＿＿＿＿＿。

〔　うる(to sell)　のむ(to drink)　着る(to wear)　持つ(to hold)　する(to do)　〕

V O C A B U L A R Y

●38ページ = page 38 ●え = picture ●みて = looking at: the て-form of みる[to look] ●ぶん = sentence ●かんせいさせなさい = complete: an imperative form of かんせいさせる[to complete] ●れい = example ●たくさん = many ●ひと = person[s] ●いわって = celebrating: the て-form of いわう[to celebrate] ●ビール = beer ●やたい = stall ●わたがし = cotton candy ●りんごあめ = candied apples ●おおきい = big: い-adjective ●ぬいぐるみ = stuffed toy animal

TASKS
タスク

(1) ちがいさがし―どこが　ちがうか？

Search for the Difference—What are the differences?　　　　　　　　【→GN❹-2】

　Aさんは　大阪に　一人で　住んで　います。　Aさんの　かぞくは　東京に
住んで　います。　Aさんの　おくさんが　東京から　来ました。　そして、Aさんの
部屋の　そうじを　しました。　〈2〉の　絵は　〈1〉の　絵と　どこが
ちがいますか。「～て　ある」を　使って　ください。

例：テーブルの　上に　花が　かざって　ある。

1　ハンガーに　ようふくが　＿＿＿＿＿＿＿＿＿＿＿。

2　れいぞうこが　＿＿＿＿＿＿＿＿＿＿＿。

3　テーブルの　上に　てがみが　＿＿＿＿＿＿＿＿＿＿＿。

4　でんきが　＿＿＿＿＿＿＿＿＿＿＿。

5　カーテンが　＿＿＿＿＿＿＿＿＿＿＿。

〔　しめる(to close)　おく(to put)　かける(to hang)　つける(to turn on)　〕

〈1〉　　　　　　　　　　　　〈2〉

(2) ガンバ探偵の 事件メモ❹—まいごを さがせ！

The Casebook of Detective Gamba ❹—Search for the Lost Child!　　　【→GN❹-1】

ガンバ探偵は 3人の おとうさん（山田さんと 小林さんと 中川さん）の
まいごを さがして います。 いっしょに さがしましょう。

山田さん
わたしの 子どもは
女の 子です。
かみは みじかいです。
ふうせんを もって います。

小林さん
わたしの 子どもは
男の 子です。
ながい ズボンを
はいています。
おもちゃを もって
います。

中川さん
わたしの 子どもは
女の 子です。
かみは ながいです。
めがねを かけて います。

山田さんの こども（　）, 小林さんの こども（　）, 中川さんの こども（　）

絵を 見て こたえましょう。

Look at the picture below and answer はい (yes) or いいえ (no).

1　山田さんの 子どもは でんわボックスの そばに います。{はい・いいえ}
2　山田さんの 子どもは 泣いて います。{はい・いいえ}
3　小林さんの 子どもは 池の そばに います。{はい・いいえ}
4　小林さんの 子どもは 犬と あそんで います。{はい・いいえ}
5　中川さんの 子どもは 本を よんで います。{はい・いいえ}
6　中川さんの 子どもは たって います。{はい・いいえ}

VOCABULARY

1

●ちがい = difference ●さがし = search ●どこ = where, which part ●ちがう = to differ ●おおさか = Osaka [the biggest city in western Japan] ●に = in, at, on: a location particle ●ひとりで = alone, by oneself ●すんで = living: the て-form of すむ[to live] ●かぞく = family ●とうきょう = Tokyo [the capital of Japan] ●から = from ●きました = came: the past tense of きます[to come]【→GN❸-1 for the past tenses】●そして = and: conjunction ●へや = room ●そうじ = cleaning ●しました = the past tense of します[to do] ●ちがいます = the polite form of ちがう above: ～と ちがいます[be different from...] ●つかって = using: the て-form of つかう[to use]: the て-form +ください indicates a polite request; i.e., つかって ください means "please use" ●テーブル = table ●うえ = on ●はな = flower ●ハンガー = hanger ●ようふく = clothes ●れいぞうこ = refrigerator ●てがみ = letter ●でんき = electric light ●カーテン = curtain

2

●たんてい = detective ●じけん = case ●メモ = memo, book ●まいご = lost child ●さがせ = search: emphatic imperative form of さがす[to search] ●さんにん = three people: さん[three]+にん[counter for person] ●おとうさん = father ●と = and ●さがして = searching: the て-form of さがす[to search] ●いっしょに = together ●さがしましょう = let's search: the verb-ましょう form means "let's" ●わたしの = my ●おんなの こ = girl ●かみ = hair ●みじかい = short: い-adjective ●ふうせん = balloon ●おとこの こ = boy ●ながい = long: い-adjective ●ズボン = pants ●はいて = wearing: the て-form of はく[to wear] ●おもちゃ = toy ●めがね = glasses ●かける = to wear, to hang ●こたえましょう = let's answer: the ましょう-form of こたえる[to answer] ●でんわボックス = telephone booth ●そば = nearby ●います = to exist: the polite form of いる[to exist]【→GN❶-4 for existential sentences】●ないて = crying: the て-form of なく[to cry] ●いけ = pond ●いぬ = dog ●と = with ●たって = standing: the て-form of たつ[to stand]

⑤ 夏休み
Summer Holiday

Most students in Japan from elementary school
age to university level have
a month-long summer holiday from late June.
Many children have lots of summer homework and
elementary school students have to keep
an illustrated diary of their holiday.
Particularly in small country communities,
students are also expected to attend daily radio-instructed
physical exercise sessions called 'rajio taisoo'.
Traditional summer pastimes are
cicada- and beetle-hunting,
but urban kids are more likely to spend the summer playing
computer games at home or hanging out with
friends at hamburger bars and amusement centers.

MAIN TEXT — ほんぶん

Look at the picture on the next page and read the following passage.

夏休み（陳さんの　日記）

今　学校は　夏休みだ。　日本では　八月が　いちばん　暑い。　暑い
日が　毎日　続く。　今日は　きのうより　暑かった。　中国の　夏も
暑い。　しかし、日本の　夏ほど　むし暑く　ない。

Summer Holiday (Ms. Chen's Summer Holiday Diary)
It's now the school summer holiday. August is the hottest time in Japan—it's hot everyday. Today
was hotter than yesterday. Summer in China is hot too, but it isn't as humid as Japan.

PRONUNCIATION　はつおん

Listen to and repeat after the tape. High and low pitches are marked with ⌐ and ⌐, and the stressed word is in bold below.

Ima gakkoo-wa **natsuyasumi**-da. Nihon-de-wa hachigatsu-ga ichiban **atsui**. Atsui
hi-ga **mainichi** tsuzuku. **Kyoo**-wa kinoo-yori atsukatta. **Chuugoku**-no natsu-mo
atsui. Shikashi, **Nihon**-no natsu-hodo mushiatsuku nai.

EXPLANATION　せつめい

The following breakdown of terms will help you to understand the passage.

① 夏休み（陳さんの　日記）

なつやすみ summer holiday: なつ[summer]+やすみ
　[holiday]
チェンさん Ms. Chen
の of: particle to indicate the noun that modifies a suc-
　ceeding noun
にっき diary

② 今　学校は　夏休みだ。

いま now
がっこう school
は as for, speaking of: particle to indicate the topic in the
　sentence 【→GN❶-4 for the topic particle は】
だ is, are: copula 【→GN❶-1, 4 for copulas】

③ 日本では　八月が　いちばん　暑い。

にほん Japan
で in, at: here, a location particle used in sentences
　without the ある／いる existential verbs
はちがつ August
が particle to indicate the subject, i.e., what is being
　talked about in the sentence 【→GN❶-4 for the
　particle が】
いちばん to the greatest degree, No. 1: used here as a
　superlative
あつい hot: い-adjective 【→GN❶-1, 2 for い-
　adjective】

④ 暑い　日が　毎日　続く。

ひ day[s]
まいにち every day
つづく to continue

⑤今日は きのうより 暑かった。

きょう today
きのう yesterday
より [more] than 【→GN❺-1】
あつかった was hot: the past tense of あつい[hot] 【→
　　GN❸-1 for the past tenses】

⑥中国の 夏も 暑い。

ちゅうごく China

も also

⑦しかし、日本の 夏ほど むし暑く
　ない。

しかし but: conjunction
ほど as much as 【→GN❺-1】
むしあつく ない not muggy: the negative form of む
　　しあつい[muggy] 【→GN❸-1 for negative
　　forms】

DIALOGUE かいわ

Did you understand the passage? In the following conversation, Ms. Chen, and Mr. Kaneda are talking about the hot summers in Japan.

陳　：今日も　暑い　ですね。

金田：ほんとに。　今が　いちばん　暑い　季節ですからね。　中国の
　　　夏は　どうですか。

陳　：中国の　夏も　暑いですが、日本の　夏ほど　むし暑く
　　　ありません。

金田：そうですか。　これから　すずしい　所へ　行きませんか。

陳　：いいですね。　どこですか。

金田：お化けやしきです。

Chen: It's hot again today, isn't it?
Kaneda: Yes—well it's the hottest time of the year now. What about summer in China?
Chen: China's summers are hot as well, but not as humid as Japan.
Kaneda: I see. Do you want to go somewhere cool?
Chen: Good idea. Where are we going?
Kaneda: To a haunted house.

Listen to and repeat after the tape. Try to imitate well when practicing this exercise.

Chen: Kyoo-mo **atsui**-desu-ne.

Kaneda: **Hontoni. Ima**-ga ichiban atsui kisetsu-desu-kara-ne. **Chuugoku**-no natsu-wa doo-desu-ka.

Chen: Chuugoku-no natsu-mo atsui-desu-ga, **Nihon**-no natsu-hodo mushiatsuku arimasen.

Kaneda: **Soo**-desu-ka. Kore-kara **suzushii** tokoro-e ikimasen-ka.

Chen: **Ii**-desu-ne. **Doko**-desu-ka.

Kaneda: **Obakeyashiki**-desu.

EXPLANATION　　せつめい

Did you understand the dialogue? If you didn't, the following breakdown of terms will help you to understand and enjoy it.

⑧ 今日も　暑い　ですね。

です is, are: copula, the polite form of だ above 【→GN ❶-1 for plain vs. polite forms】

ね isn't it true!: particle used at the end of a sentence for confirmation or exclamation

⑨ ほんとに。今が　いちばん　暑い 季節ですからね。

ほんとに indeed, really

きせつ season, time of the year

から because, for: conjunction

⑩ 中国の　夏は　どうですか。

どう how are

か question particle used at the end of a sentence

⑪ 中国の　夏も　暑いですが、日本の 夏ほど　むし暑く　ありません。

が but: conjunction 【→GN❸-2 for the conjunction が】

むしあつく ありません not muggy: the polite form of

むしあつく ない, above 【→GN❸-1 for negative forms, GN❺-1】

⑫ そうですか。これから　すずしい 所へ　行きませんか。

そうですか Is that right?

これから from now on

すずしい cool: い-adjective

ところ place

へ to: particle to indicate directions 【→GN❷-1 for related expressions】

いきませんか Would you like to go?: negative questions are often used to imply an invitation

⑬ いいですね。どこですか。

いい good: い-adjective

どこ where

⑭ お化けやしきです。

おばけやしき haunted house [Japanese enjoy visiting haunted houses in amusement parks—especially in the summer.]

GRAMMAR NOTES (GN❺)
ぶんぽうノート

【GN❺-1】

Comparison. Below are some typical sentences of comparison. Sentence (1) with より (than), is the affirmative comparative; sentence (2), with ほど(to the extent of), is the negative comparative; sentence (3), with いちばん (to the greatest degree, No.1) is the superlative form. In a comparative sentence like (1), (の)ほう (the alternative) may not be used (as in ⑤). (Note that (1) and (2) share the same meaning.)

【→ Drill 1, 2, Task 1, 2】

（１）この 橋（の ほう）が あの 橋より 広い。
　　　This bridge is wider than that bridge.

（２）あの 橋は この 橋ほど 広く ない。
　　　That bridge is not as wide as this bridge.

（３）京都では この お寺が いちばん 大きい。
　　　In Kyoto, this temple is the biggest.

Refer also to Main Text and Dialogue sentences ⑤, ⑦, ⑪, ③, and ⑨, which are rewritten below.

⑤今日は きのうより 暑かった。

⑦しかし、日本の 夏ほど むし暑く ない。

⑪中国の 夏も 暑いですが、日本の 夏ほど むし暑く ありません。

③日本では 八月が いちばん 暑い。

⑨今が いちばん 暑い 季節ですからね。

The following pairs of adjectival opposites will be useful for comparison.

暑い (hot) —— 寒い (cold)

高い (expensive) —— 安い (cheap)

重い (heavy) —— 軽い (light)

速い (fast) —— 遅い (slow)

せまい (narrow) —— 広い (wide)

大きい (big) —— 小さい (small)

むずかしい (difficult) —— やさしい (easy)

暖かい (warm) —— 涼しい (cool)

高い (tall) —— 低い (low)

新しい (new) —— 古い (old)

長い (long) —— 短い (short)

おいしい (delicious) —— まずい (unpleasant tasting)

多い (many, much) —— 少ない (few, little)

ドリル

（１）絵を　見て、文を　かんせいさせなさい。

Look at the illustrations, and complete the sentences. Choose the correct adjectives.

【→GN❺-1】

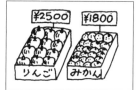

例：りんごの　ほうが　みかんより　高い。

1　本通りの　ほうが　並木通りより　＿＿＿＿＿＿。

2　まぐろは　たいより　＿＿＿＿＿＿。

3　鈴木さんの　にもつは　田中さんの　にもつほど　＿＿＿＿＿＿。

4　張さんの　かみは　陳さんの　かみほど　＿＿＿＿＿＿。

5　漢字と　ひらがなと　カタカナの　中で　漢字が　いちばん　＿＿＿＿＿＿。

（２）はんたいの　いみの　ペアを　さがしなさい。

Find pairs of words that are opposite in meaning.

【→GN❺-1】

①低い　　②すずしい　　③むずかしい　　④まずい　　⑤すくない　　⑥高い

⑦多い　　⑧やさしい　　⑨あたたかい　　⑩おいしい

V O C A B U L A R Y

1

●え = picture ●みて = looking at: the て-form of みる[to look at] ●ぶん = sentence ●かんせいさせなさい = complete: an imperative form of かんせいさせる[to complete] ●りんご = apple ●みかん = mandarin orange ● ほんどおり = Hon-doori [a street] ●なみきどおり = Namiki-doori ●まぐろ = tuna ●たい = sea bream ●にもつ = luggage ●かみ = hair ●かんじ = kanji: Chinese characters ●なかで = among

2

●はんたい = opposite ●いみ = meaning ●ペア = pair ●さがしなさい = look for: an imperative form of さがす[to look for]

TASKS
タスク

(1) お元気ですか？―はがきさがし

How are you?—Postcard Search　　　　　　　　　　　【→GN❺-1，GN❹-1，GN❸-1】

金田さんは　友だちの　高橋さんと　山へ　キャンプに　行きました。　そして、
友だちの　陳さんに　はがきを　出しました。　どちらの　はがきが　金田さんの
はがきでしょう？

金田さん　　高橋さん

（A）	（B）
陳さん、お元気ですか。　ぼくは　今　高橋さんと　いっしょに　山の　中に　います。ぼくたちは　いちばん　小さい　テントを　使って　います。　今日　川で　さかなつりを　しました。　高橋さんの　さかなが　ぼくの　さかなより　すこし　大きかったです。 　　　　　　　　　　8月3日　金田　洋	陳さん、お元気ですか。　ぼくは　今　高橋さんと　いっしょに　山で　夏休みを　すごして　います。ぼくたちの　テントは　とても　小さい　テントです。　今日　みずうみで　さかなを　つりました。　ぼくの　さかなの　ほうが　高橋さんの　さかなより　大きかったです。 　　　　　　　　　　8月3日　金田　洋

(2) ガンバ探偵の 事件メモ❺─3億円を 探せ！

The Casebook of Detective Gamba ❺—Search for 300 Million Yen!

【→GN❺-1,GN❹-1, GN❶-3, GN❶-4】

ここに 古い 手紙と 地図が あります。手紙には 3億円の かくし場所が
書いて あります。 ガンバ探偵は その 場所を すぐ 見つけました。
さて、どこでしょう？

この 町には 川が 二つ ある。
大きい ほうの 川の 橋は さかえ橋と ともえ橋だ。
さかえ橋の ほうが ともえ橋より 広い。
さかえ橋の 近くにも お寺が ある。
この 町で いちばん 大きい お寺だ。
この お寺の まわりに 木が 三本 ある。
3億円は いちばん 低い 木の 下に ある。

V O C A B U L A R Y

1

●おげんきですか = How are you? ●はがき = postcard ●さがし = search ●ともだち = friend[s] ●たかはしさん = Mr. Takahashi ●と = with ●キャンプ = camp ●に = for, to: here, particle to indicate a purpose or goal ●いきました = went: the polite past tense of いく [to go] ●そして = and: conjunction ●を = particle to indicate the [direct] object【→GN❷-1 for the particle を】●だしました = sent: the polite past tense of だす [to send] ●どちら = which one [of the two] ●でしょう = is likely to be: uncertain version of です ●ぼく = I [masculine] ●いっしょに = together ●やま = mountain ●なか = inside ●に = in: here, a location particle ●います = to stay: the polite form of いる [to stay] ●ぼくたち = we [masculine] ●テント = tent ●つかって います = is using: the polite て いる form of つかう [to use]【→GN❹-1 for the て/で いる form】●かわ = river ●で = in, at: here, a location particle ●さかなつり = fishing: さかな [fish]+つり [fishing] ●しました = did: the polite past tense of する [to do] ●すこし = a little ●おおきかった = was big: the past tense of おおきい [big] ●すごして います = is spending: the polite て いる form of すごす [to spend] ●とても = very ●みずうみ = lake ●つりました = fished: the polite past tense of つる [to fish] ●はちがつ = August ●みっか = the third of the month

2

●たんてい = detective ●じけん = case ●メモ = memo, book ●さんおくえん = 300 million yen ●さがせ = search: emphatic imperative form of さがす ●ここ = here ●てがみ = letter ●ちず = map ●あります = there is, to exist: the polite form of ある [to exist] ●かくしばしょ = hidden location: かくし [hiding]+ばしょ [place] ●かいて あります = is written: the polite て ある form of かく [to write]【→GN❹-2 for the て/で ある form】●その = that __ ●すぐ = soon ●みつけました = found: the polite past tense of みつける [to find] ●さて = well ●どこ = where ●まち = town ●ふたつ = two [things] ●ある = to exist ●さかえばし = Sakae Bridge ●ともえばし = Tomoe Bridge ●ちかく = nearby ●おてら = temple ●まわり = around ●き = tree ●さんぼん = さん [three]+ほん [counter for long, cylindrical objects] ●した = under

❻月見と　台風
（つきみ）　　　（たいふう）

Moon-viewing and Typhoons

Tsukimi, or moon-viewing, has long been a popular autumn pastime and,
like flower-viewing, a common theme in literature and the arts.
Following Chinese customs and rather like Thanksgiving,
Japanese moon-viewing consists of making offerings of beans,
fruit and the like to the full (harvest) moon while admiring its beauty from the veranda or garden.
The fall-flowering *susuki* grass is used for decoration,
and is a common companion to the moon in paintings.
Today, moon-viewing is not as popular as flower-viewing, partly because not many city dwellers
have suitable gardens or verandas, but it still has a very romantic image.
Typhoons, on the other hand, are anything but romantic.
These whirling storms tear through Japan and other islands in the Pacific,
wreaking havok and destruction from August through October.
Not all the tempest is bad, through, since their strong winds have twice
in history prevented Mongolian invasions of Japan.

MAIN TEXT — ほんぶん

Look at the picture below and read the following passage.

月見と　台風

きのうは　いい　天気だった。　木村さんの　うちで　お月見を
した。　きれいな　月だった。　しかし、今日は　風が　強い。
台風が　近づいて　いるそうだ

Moon-viewing and Typhoons
It was a fine day yesterday. I went moon-viewing at the home of Mr. Kimura. The moon was beautiful. Today though is very windy. I hear that a typhoon is on the way.

Listen to and repeat after the tape. High and low pitches are marked with ⌐ and ⌐ , and the stressed word is in bold below.

Kinoo-wa **ii** tenki-datta. Kimura-san-no uchi-de o-**tsukimi**-o shita. **Kireena** tsuki-datta. Shikashi, kyoo-wa **kaze**-ga tsuyoi. **Taifuu**-ga chikazuite-iru-soo-da.

EXPLANATION せつめい

The following breakdown of terms will help you to understand the passage.

① 月見と　台風

つきみ moon-viewing: moon[つき]-viewing[み]
と and: particle
たいふう typhoon

② きのうは　いい　天気だった。

きのう yesterday
は as for, speaking of: particle to indicate the topic in the sentence 【→GN❶-4 for the topic particle は】
いい good: い-adjective 【→GN❶-2 for い-adjective】
てんき weather
だった was, were: copula, the past tense of だ [is, are] 【→GN❸-1 for a summary on the past tense of the predicate】

③ 木村さんの　うちでお月見を　した。

きむらさん Mr. Kimura
の of: particle to indicate the noun that modifies a succeeding noun
うち house, home
で at, in, on: particle to indicate a location where an action takes place
お prefix to make つきみ a more polite expression

を particle to indicate the [direct] object of the verb 【→GN❷-1 for the particle を】
した did : the past tense of する [to do]

④ きれいな　月だった。

きれいな attractive: な-adjective 【→GN❶-2 for な-adjective】
つき moon

⑤ しかし、今日は　風が　強い。

しかし but, however: conjunction
きょう today
かぜ wind
が particle to indicate the subject,i.e., what is being talked about in the sentence 【→GN❶-4 for the particle が】
つよい strong: い-adjective

⑥ 台風が　近づいて　いるそうだ。

ちかづいて いる is approaching : the て いる form of ちかづく [to approach] 【→GN❹-1 for the て／で+いる form】
そうだ I hear 【→GN❻-1】

DIALOGUE — かいわ

Did you understand the passage? In the following conversation, Ms. Cooper and Mr. Kimura are talking about moon-viewing and the typhoon.

クーパー：きのうの　お月見（つきみ）楽（たの）しかったです。

　　　　　ありがとう　ございました。

木村（きむら）　：いいえ、どういたしまして。

クーパー：今日（きょう）は　風（かぜ）が　強（つよ）いですね。

木村　　：ええ。　雨（あめ）も　ふりそうですね。

クーパー：台風（たいふう）が　近（ちか）づいて　いるそうですよ。　こわいですね。

木村　　：ええ。　でも、うちの　かないは　もっと　こわいです。

Cooper: Thank you for the wonderful moon-viewing party yesterday.
Kimura: I'm glad you enjoyed it.
Cooper: It's windy today, isn't it?
Kimura: Yes, and it looks like rain.
Cooper: Apparently there's a typhoon on the way. Scary, isn't it?
Kimura: Mmm, but not as scary as my wife!

Listen to and repeat after the tape. Try to imitate well when practicing this exercise.

Cooper: Kinoo-no o-tsukimi **tanoshikatta**-desu. **Arigatoo** gozaimashita.

Kimura: **Iie**, doo-itashimashite.

Cooper: Kyoo-wa **kaze**-ga tsuyoi-desu-ne.

Kimura: Ee. **Ame**-mo furi-soo-desu-ne.

Cooper: **Taifuu**-ga chikazuite-iru-soo-desu-yo. **Kowai**-desu-ne.

Kimura: Ee. Demo, uchi-no **kanai**-wa motto kowai-desu.

EXPLANATION せつめい

Did you understand the passage? If you didn't, the following breakdown of terms will help you to understand and enjoy it.

⑦ きのうの　お月見　楽しかったです。
　 ありがとう　ございました。

たのしかった was enjoyable: the past tense of たのし
　 い、い-adjective
です is, are: copula, the polite form of だ【→GN❶-1
　 for だ and です difference】
ありがとう ございました Thank you [for what you've
　 done for me].

⑧ いいえ、どういたしまして。

いいえ、どういたしまして Not at all. Don't mention
　 it. いいえ [no] is optional.

⑨ 今日は　風が　強いですね。

ね isn' it?: used at the end of a sentence for confirmation
　 or exclamation

⑩ ええ。雨も　ふりそうですね。

ええ yes: more informal than はい

あめ rain
も also: particle
ふりそう looks like rain【→GN❻-1】

⑪ 台風が　近づいて　いるそうですよ。
　 こわいですね。

そうです I hear: the polite form of そうだ above
よ you know: particle used at the end of a sentence for
　 emphasis
こわい frightening, scary: い-adjective

⑫ ええ。でも、うちの　かないは
　 もっと　こわいです。

でも but:conjunction, more informal than しかし
かない [my] wife
もっと more【→GN❺-1 for comparative sentences】
(This sentence, of course, is a joke!)

GRAMMAR NOTES (GN❻)
ぶんぽうノート

【GN❻-1】

The plain form＋そう（だ／です）means "I hear that..." "They say that...," as in sentence (1). But, as in sentence (2), そう（だ／です）, when attached to the bound form (i.e., ます-dropped form) of the verb or the stems of い-adjective and な-adjective, means "it looks (like)..." "It seems that...," a conjecture (guess) based on one's observation or feelings.【→ GN❸-1 for different forms of the predicate】

【→ Drill 1, 2, Task 1, 2】

（１）雨が　ふる＋そうだ。

    I hear／They say that it's going to rain.

（２）雨が　ふり＋そうだ。

    It looks like it's going to rain.　(Note: ふり ← ふります)

Compare the two different forms to which そうだ／です are attached.

	plain form	＋そうだ／です (hearsay)	＋そうだ／です (conjecture)
verb い-adjective な-adjective noun	近づく 楽しい 元気だ (to be healthy, well) 台風だ	近づく 楽しい 元気だ 台風だ	近づき（←近づきます） 楽し 元気 ――――

Refer also to sentences ⑥, ⑪, and ⑩ in the Main Text and the Dialogue.

⑥台風が　近づいて　いるそうだ。

⑪台風が　近づいて　いるそうですよ。

⑩雨も　ふりそうですね。

Note that the negative conjecture and the conjecture of いい (good) are somewhat irregular.

【→ GN❷-2, GN❸-1 for negative sentences】

雨は　ふらなさそうです。

（←ふらない [to not rain]）It looks like it's not going to rain.

この　大学は　よさそうです。

This university looks good.

DRILLS

ドリル

（１）表を　かんせいさせなさい。

Complete the chart.　　　　　　　　　　　　　　　　　　　　　　　【→GN❻-1】

plain, dictionary form	hearsay (I hear that...)	conjecture (It looks [like]...)
はれる(to clear up)	はれるそうだ	（１　　　　）そうだ
強い(to be strong)	（２　　　　）そうだ	強そうだ
しずかだ(to be quiet)	しずかだそうだ	（３　　　　）そうだ
天気だ(to be fine weather)	（４　　　　）そうだ	――

（２）下の　文を　a‐dと　組み合わせて　かんせいさせなさい。

Complete the sentences, using the words below.　　　　　　　　　　【→GN❻-1】

1　オーストラリアの　友だちから　手紙が　来た。

　　オーストラリアは　今 ＿＿＿＿＿＿＿。

2　星が　きれいだ。　あしたも ＿＿＿＿＿＿＿。

3　テレビの　天気よほうに　よると　あさっては　雨が ＿＿＿＿＿＿＿。

4　伊藤さんは　このまえ　おかあさんを　なくした。　今　とても ＿＿＿＿＿＿＿。

（ａ）さびしそうだ（←さびしい）　　（ｂ）寒いそうだ（←寒い）

（ｃ）ふるそうだ（←ふる）　　（ｄ）はれそうだ（←はれる）

VOCABULARY

1
●ひょう＝chart ●かんせいさせなさい＝complete: imperative form of かんせいさせる[to complete]
2
●した＝below ●ぶん＝sentence ●～と くみあわせて＝combining with...: the て‐form of ～と くみあわせる[to combine with...] ●オーストラリア＝Australia ●ともだち＝friend ●から＝from ●てがみ＝letter ●きた＝came: the past tense of くる[to come] ●いま＝now ●ほし＝star ●あした＝tomorrow ●テレビ＝TV ●よほう＝forecast ●～に よると＝according to... ●あさって＝the day after tomorrow ●いとうさん＝Mr./Ms. Ito ●このまえ＝the other day ●おかあさん＝mother ●なくした＝lost: the past tense of なくす[to lose] ●とても＝very ●さびしい＝lonely: い‐adjective ●さむい＝cold: い‐adjective ●ふる＝to rain

TASKS
タスク

(1) あしたの　天気は？

What about tomorrow's weather?

【→GN❻-1, GN❹-1】

花子さんと　雪子さんが　電話で　話しを　して　います。花子さんと　雪子さんは
どこに　住んで　いるか　考えて　ください。

花子：そちらの　天気は　どうですか。
雪子：こちらは　今　くもって　います。あしたは　雨が　ふりそうです。
花子：天気よほうに　よると　そちらの　雨の　確率は　60％だそうですよ。
雪子：そうですか。　そちらは　どうですか。
花子：こちらも　今　くもっていますが、あしたは　はれそうです。こちらの
　　　雨の　確率は　10％です。あしたの　最高気温は　20度だそうです。

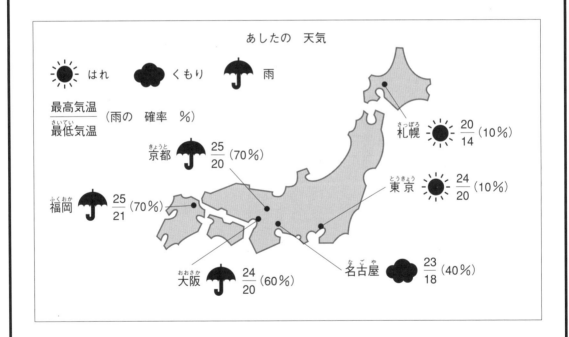

花子さん（　　　）　雪子さん（　　　）

(2) ガンバ探偵の 事件メモ ❻ ―住人さがし

The Casebook of Detective Gamba ❻―Resident Search 　　　　【→GN❻-1, GN❹-1】

アパートの 102号室の 山口さんが 殺されました。203号室は 空き室です。
ガンバ探偵と いっしょに 101～202号室の 住人の リストを 作って ください。

小川：山口さんの となりの へやの 石田さんは 大阪 出身だそうですよ。

　　　石田さんは 公務員だそうです。

上田：わたしは 山口さんの 上に 住んで います。 となりは 中山さんです。

　　　名古屋で 生まれたそうです。 車の セールスマンだそうですよ。

中山：小川さんの 上に 住んで います。 小川さんは 札幌から 来たそうです。

　　　となりは 上田さんです。上田さんの ふるさとは 福岡だそうです。

石田：小川さんは 山口さんの となりに 住んで います。 カメラマンだそうです。

　　　上田さんですか？ 高校で 英語を 教えて いるそうです。

部屋番号	101	102	103	201	202	203
名前	(a)	山口	(d)	(g)	(j)	空き室
出身	(b)	京都	(e)	(h)	(k)	
仕事	(c)	銀行員	(f)	(i)	(l)	

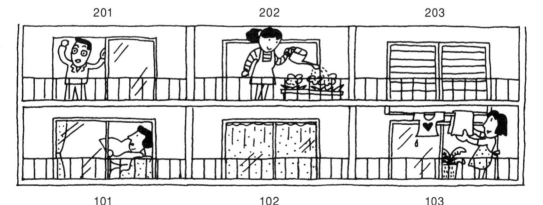

名前：(1)石田　(2)中山　(3)小川　(4)上田
出身：(5)大阪　(6)名古屋　(7)札幌　(8)福岡
仕事：(9)公務員　(10)セールスマン　(11)カメラマン　(12)先生

1

●はなこ, ゆきこ are both common women's names. ●でんわ = telephone ●で = by means of: here, an instrumental particle ●はなし = talk ●して います = is doing: the polite 〜て いる form of する[to do] ●どこ = where ●に = at, in: here, a location particle ●すんで いる is living/lives: the 〜で いる form of すむ[to live] ●かんがえて ください = please think: the polite request form of かんがえる[to think] ●そちら = that [your] place ●どう = how ●こちら = this [our] place ●くもって います = is cloudy: the polite 〜て いる form of くもる[to cloud] ●が = but: here, conjunction【→GN ❸-2 for the conjunction が】●ど = degrees: temperature ●さっぽろ, とうきょう, なごや, きょうと, おおさか, ふくおか are all big cities in Japan. ●はれ = clear weather ●さいこう = highest ●きおん = temperature ●さいてい = lowest ●かくりつ = probability

2

●たんてい = detective ●じけん = case ●メモ = memo, book ●じゅうにん = resident ●さがし = search ●アパート = apartment house ●ごうしつ = room number ●やまぐち, いしだ, なかやま, おがわ, うえだ are all common family names. ●ころされました = was killed: the polite passive past tense of ころす[to kill]【→⓫-1 for passive sentences】●あきしつ = vacant apartment ●〜と いっしょに = together with... ●リスト = list ●つくって ください = please make: the polite request form of つくる[to make] ●となり = next door ●へや = room ●しゅっしん = where one is from ●こうむいん = public employee ●わたし = I ●うえ = above, on ●すんで います = is living / lives: the polite form of すんで いる above ●うまれた = was born: the past tense of うまれる[to be born] ●くるま = car ●セールスマン = salesman ●ふるさと = hometown ●カメラマン = photographer ●こうこう = high school ●えいご = English ●おしえて いる = is teaching / teaches: the 〜て いる form of おしえる[to teach] ●ばんごう = number ●なまえ = name ●しごと = job, occupation ●ぎんこういん = bank clerk ●せんせい = teacher

❼ スポーツ
Sports

Spectator and leisure sports alike are very popular in Japan,
partly because they embody admired values
like team spirit and perseverence.
The salaryman's favored spectator sports
seem to be baseball and *sumoo*,
while young people prefer soccer or baseball.
In their spare time, middle-aged men in particular like a spot of golf,
while their sons and daughters prefer tennis or skiing.
In the post-war period, Japan has hosted
many important sporting events,
notably the 1964 Tokyo Olympic Games,
and almost all schools, universities and
companies have sports clubs.
The current sports crazes are soccer and snowboarding.

MAIN TEXT — ほんぶん

Look at the picture on the next page and read the following passage.

スポーツ

陳さんは　スポーツが　好きだ。　最近、テニスを　始めた。
テニススクールに　通って　いるが、まだ　へただ。　金田さんは
テニスが　じょうずだ。　陳さんは　金田さんと　テニスを
したがって　いる。

Sports
Ms. Chen likes sports. She recently started to play tennis. She goes to tennis school, but she isn't very good yet. Mr. Kaneda is good at tennis, and Ms. Chen wants to play with him.

PRONUNCIATION　はつおん

Listen to and repeat after the tape. High and low pitches are marked with 「 and 」, and the stressed word is in bold below.

Chen-san-wa **supootsu**-ga suki-da. Saikin, **tenisu**-o hajimeta. Tenisu-sukuuru-ni kayotte iru-ga, mada **heta**-da. Kaneda-san-wa tenisu-ga **joozu**-da. Chen-san-wa **Kaneda**-san-to tenisu-o shitagatte iru.

EXPLANATION　せつめい

The following breakdown of terms will help you to understand the passage.

① スポーツ

スポーツ sport[s]

② 陳さんは　スポーツが　好きだ。

チェンさん Ms. Chen

は as for, speaking of: particle to indicate the topic in the sentence 【→GN❶-4 for the topic particle は】

が particle to indicate the object, here 【→GN❼-1】, although が usually indicate the subject of the sentence. 【→GN❶-4 for the subject particle が】

すき be fond of, to like: な-adjective 【→GN❶-2 for な-adjective】

だ is, are: copula 【→GN❸-1 for a summary on Japanese predicates】

③ 最近、テニスを　始めた。

さいきん recently

テニス tennis

を particle to indicate the [direct] object of the verb 【→GN❷-1 for the particle を】

はじめた began: the past tense of はじめる[to begin] 【→GN❸-1 for a summary on the past tense of the predicates】

④ テニススクールに　通って　いるが、まだ　へただ。

スクール school

に to: particle to indicate a location or a goal

かよって いる is going [commuting] to: the て いる form of かよう [to go to, to commute] 【→GN❹-1 for the て／で いる／います form】

が but: here, conjunction 【→GN❸-2 for the conjunction が】

まだ yet, still

へた unskilled, not good at: な -adjective 【→GN❼-1】

⑤金田さんは　テニスが　じょうずだ。

かねださん Mr. Kaneda

じょうず skillful, good at: な -adjective 【→GN❼-1】

⑥陳さんは　金田さんと　テニスを
　したがって　いる。

と with: particle

したがって いる want to do: the たがって いる form of する [to do] 【→GN❼-2】

DIALOGUE — かいわ

Did you understand the passage? In the following conversation, Mr. Kaneda and Ms. Chen are talking about sports, particularly about playing tennis.

金田：テニスを　始めたそうですね。

陳　：ええ。　でも、まだ　へたです。

金田：ほかに　どんな　スポーツが　好きですか。

陳　：スポーツは　なんでも　好きです。　金田さんは　テニスが

　　　じょうずだそうですね。

金田：まあ、昔から　やって　いますから。

陳　：こんど　ぜひ　いっしょに　テニスが　したいです。

　　　いろいろ　教えて　ください。

金田：いいですよ、もちろん。

Kaneda: So you've started playing tennis.
Chen: Yes, but I'm not very good yet.
Kaneda: What other sports do you like?
Chen: I like them all. I hear you're good at tennis, Mr. Kaneda.
Kaneda: Well, I've been doing it for a while.
Chen: I really want to play a game with you soon. Please give me some tips.
Kaneda: That's fine by me.

Listen to and repeat after the tape. Try to imitate well when practicing this exercise.

Kaneda: **Tenisu**-o hajimeta-soo-desu-ne.

Chen: Ee. Demo, mada **heta**-desu.

Kaneda: Hokani **donna** supootsu-ga suki-desu-ka.

Chen: Supootsu-wa **nandemo** suki-desu. Kaneda-san-wa tenisu-ga **joozu**-da-soo-desu-ne.

Kaneda: Maa, **mukashi**-kara yatte imasu-kara.

Chen: Kondo zehi **isshoni** tenisu-ga shitai-desu. Iroiro **oshiete** kudasai.

Kaneda: **Ii**-desu-yo, mochiron.

EXPLANATION　せつめい

Did you understand the conversation? If you didn't, the following breakdown of terms will help you to understand and enjoy it.

⑦ テニスを　始めたそうですね。

そう I hear 【→GN❻-1 for a summary on そう】
です copula: the polite form of だ above
ね isn't it true!: used at the end of a sentence for confirmation or exclamation

⑧ ええ。でも、まだ　へたです。

ええ yes: more informal than はい
でも but, however: here, conjunction

⑨ ほかに　どんな　スポーツが
　好きですか。

ほかに besides [that]
どんな what kind of
か question particle used at the end of a sentence

⑩ スポーツは　なんでも　好きです。
　金田さんは　テニスが
　じょうずだそうですね。

なんでも anything

⑪ まあ、昔から　やって　いますから。

まあ well, say
むかし early [old] times, long ago
から from, since: particle

やって います is doing: the て います form of やる
　　[to do], a synonym for する[to do]
から because: here, conjunction

⑫ こんど　ぜひ　いっしょに
　テニスが　したいです。

こんど another [next] time
ぜひ by all means
いっしょに together
したい want to do: the たい-form of する[to do] 【→
　GN❼-2】

⑬ いろいろ　教えて　ください。

いろいろ many things
おしえて teaching: the て-form of おしえる[to teach]
　【→GN❹-1 for the て-form】
ください the て-form+ください means a polite request:
　therefore、おしえて　ください means 'Please teach.'

⑭ いいですよ、もちろん。

いい fine, O.K., good: い-adjective 【→GN❶-1, 2 for
　い-adjective】
よ I tell you, you know: particle used at the end of a
　sentence for emphasis
もちろん of course

GRAMMAR NOTES (GN❼)
ぶんぽうノート

【GN❼-1】
な -adjectives such as 好き(be fond of, to like)、きらい(to dislike, to hate)、じょうず(skillful, good at)、へた (unskillful, not good at) are often used in the following sentence pattern (Note that が marks the object in this type of sentence):　　　　　　　　　　　　　　　　　　　　　　　　　　　　　　【→ Drill 1, Task 1, 2】

$$\boxed{\text{TOPIC}} \text{— は} \quad \boxed{\text{OBJECT}} \text{— が 好き／きらい／じょうず／へた ＋ だ／です}$$

Sentences in the Main Text and the Dialogue which are based on this sentence pattern:

②陳さんは　スポーツが　**好きだ**。
④テニススクールに　通っているが、まだ　**へただ**。
⑨ほかに　どんな　スポーツが　**好きですか**。
⑤金田さんは　テニスが　**じょうずだ**。
⑩金田さんは　テニスが　**じょうずだそうですね**。

【GN❼-2】
The bound form (i.e., ます-dropped form) of the verb ＋たい／たいです(to want to...) is used for the first person (and for the second person in interrogative sentences) to express a personal desire to do something. For the third person, who is equal or inferior to the speaker, ＋たがって いる／います(lit. to show a sign of wanting to...) is usually used instead of ＋たい／たいです. As shown below, the object is marked with が or を in the たい／たいですsentence and always with を in the たがって いる／います sentence. (Note that たい conjugates just like an い-adjective.) 【→GN❻-1 for the bound form of the verb, →GN❸-1 for the conjugation of い-adjective】　　　　　　　　　　　　　　　　　　　　　　【→ Drill 1, 2, Task 1, 2】

（1）わたしは　水が／を　飲みたいです。I want to drink [some] water.
（2）あなたも　水が／を　飲みたいですか。Do you want to drink [some] water, too?
（3）木村さんは　水を　飲みたがって　います。Mr. Kimura wants to drink [some] water.

Refer also to sentences ⑫ and ⑥ in the Dialogue and the Main Text.

⑫こんど　ぜひ　いっしょに　テニスが　したいです。
⑥陳さんは　金田さんと　テニスを　したがって　いる。

Related to these sentences are ほしい／ほしいです and ほしがって いる／います (to want) expressions like the following (Note that only が may be used for the object in the ほしい／ほしいです sentence):

（1）わたしは　車が　ほしいです。I want a car.
（2）あなたも　車が　ほしいですか。Do you want a car, too?
（3）木村さんは　車を　ほしがって　います。Mr. Kimura wants a car.

DRILLS

ドリル

（1）正しいほうを　選びなさい。

Choose the correct answer based on the Main Text and the Dialogue.　　　　【→GN❼-1, 2】

1　（陳さん・金田さん）は　最近　テニスを　始めた。

2　（陳さん・金田さん）は　昔から　テニスを　して　いる。

3　金田さんは　テニスが　（じょうずだ・へただ）

4　陳さんは　金田さんと　テニスを　（したい・したがって　いる）

（2）「〜たい」を　使って、「雪子さんの　夢」の　文を　完成させなさい。

Complete the following sentences on "Yukiko's Dream," using the たい-forms.　　【→GN❼-2】

1　わたしは　たくさん　お金を　（　　　　　　　　　）。

2　そして、　オーストラリアへ　（　　　　　　　　　）。

3　オーストラリアで　日本語を　（　　　　　　　　　）。

4　すてきな　人と　（　　　　　　　　　）。

5　大きい　家に　（　　　　　　　　　）。

〔　教える(to teach)　ためる(to save)　住む(to live)　行く(to go)　結婚する(to marry)　〕

❖VOCABULARY❖

1
●ただしい= correct: い-adjective ●ほう = alternative ●えらびなさい = choose: an imperative form of えらぶ [to choose]
2
●つかって = using: the て-form of つかう[to use]●ゆきこ = Yukiko: common woman's name ● の = of: particle to indicate the noun that modifies a succeeding noun ●ゆめ = dream ●ぶん = sentence ●かんせいさせなさい = complete: an imperative form of かんせいさせる[to complete]●たくさん = much, many ●おかね = money ●そして = and [then]: conjunction ●オーストラリア = Australia ●へ = to: a directional particle ●で = in, at: particle to indicate the location where an action takes place ●にほんご = the Japanese language ●すてきな = wonderful: な-adjective ●ひと = person ●おおきい = big, large: い-adjective ●いえ = house

TASKS
タスク

(1) 夢の デート

Dream Dates

【→GN**7**-1, 2, GN**4**-1】

若い 男女が デートを したがって います。 だれと だれが いい カップルで
しょうか。

（A）
スポーツマンの 男の 人が 好きです。
今 テニススクールで テニスを 習って
います。 コンサートは あまり
行きませんが、カラオケは よく
行きます。 でも、おんち です。

（B）
旅行が 好きです。 いろいろな 温泉へ
行きたいです。 だから、車の 免許が
ほしいです。 料理も 大好きです。
たばこは きらいです。

（C）
車の 運転が 好きです。
休みには テニスが
したいです。 おいしい
料理も 食べたいです。
酒は 飲みません。
たばこも すいません。

（D）
スポーツは どれも
へたです。 読書が
好きです。温泉も
好きです。 車は
持って いません。
たばこは すいますが、
酒は 飲みません。

（E）
スポーツは なんでも
好きです。 テニスも
ゴルフも やりますが、
テニスの ほうが
じょうずです。 酒も
カラオケも 好きです。

(2) ガンバ探偵の 事件メモ❼―留守番電話の なぞ

The Casebook of Detective Gamba ❼—Mystery of the Answering Machine

【→GN❼-1, 2, GN❹-1】

マンションの 自分の 部屋で レストラン経営者の
山田さんが 死んで いました。 留守番電話に
メッセージが 入って いました。 だれからの
メッセージでしょうか。

山田さん、このあいだ チケットを ほしがって
いましたね。 その チケットが 2枚 手に入りました。
いっしょに ビールを 飲みながら、応援しましょう。
今年は ぜひ 優勝して ほしいですね。
また あした 電話します。

〔山田さんの 友だち〕

小川さん
ゴルフ仲間です。
映画が とても 好きです。

中山さん
レストランの お客さんです。
クラシック音楽が 好きです。

佐藤さん
近くの すし屋さんです。
野球が 大好きです。

VOCABULARY

1

●デート = date ●わかい = young: い-adjective ●だんじょ = men and women ●だれ = who ●カップル = couple ●でしょう = will probably be: uncertain version of です ●スポーツマン = sportsman ●おとこ = man ●いま = now ●ならって います = is learning: the polite て いる form of ならう[to learn] ●コンサート = concert ●あまり +negative: not often, not much ●いきません = not to go: the polite negative of いく[to go] ●カラオケ = karaoke music ●よく = often ●おんち = one who has no ear for music ●りょこう = travel ●いろいろな = various: な-adjective ●おんせん = hot spring [resort] ●だから = so, therefore: conjunction ●くるま = car ●めんきょ = license ●りょうり = cooking, dish ●だいすき = to like a lot: な-adjective ●たばこ = cigarette ●きらい = to dislike, to hate: な-adjective ●うんてん = driving ●やすみ = holiday ●に = in, during: here, particle to indicate time ●おいしい = delicious: い-adjective ●たべたい = want to eat: the たい-form of たべる[to eat] ●さけ = sake or any alchoholic beverage ●も = also: particle ●のみません = not to drink [or smoke]: the polite negative of のむ[to drink] ●どれも = any, all ●どくしょ = reading [books] ●もって いません = not to have: the polite negative て いる form of もつ[to have] ●すいます = the polite form of すう[to smoke, to inhale] ●ゴルフ = golf ●やります = to do, to play: the polite form of やる[to do] ●ほう = the alternative【→GN❺-1 for comparative sentences】

2

●たんてい = detective ●じけん = case ●メモ = memo, book ●るすばんでんわ = answering machine [phone] ●なぞ = mystery ●マンション = apartment house ●じぶん = oneself ●へや = room ●レストラン = restaurant ●けいえいしゃ = manager ●やまださん = Mr./Ms. Yamada ●しんで いました = was dead: the past polite で いる form of しぬ [to die] ●メッセージ = message ●はいって いました = was recorded: the past polite て いる form of はいる[to enter] ●このあいだ = the other day ●チケット = ticket ●その __ てにはいりました = got: the past polite form of てにはいる[to be obtained] ●ビール = beer ●のみながら = while drinking: ながら attached to the bound form [here, のみます to drink] of the verb means 'while.' ●おうえんしましょう = let's cheer: the ましょう[let's] form of おうえんする[to cheer, to root for] ●ことし = this year ●ゆうしょうして ほしい = want them to win the championship: the て ほしい[want someone to do...] form of ゆうしょうする[to win the championship] ●また = again ●あした = tomorrow ●でんわします = the polite form of でんわする[to telephone] ●ともだち = friend[s] ●おがわさん = Mr./Ms. Ogawa ●なかま = friend, colleague ●えいが = movie ●とても = very[much] ●なかやまさん = Mr./Ms. Nakayama ●おきゃくさん = guest, customer ●クラシックおんがく = classical music ●さとうさん = Mr./Ms. Sato ●ちかく = nearby ●すしやさん = sushi chef

⑧ 紅葉
こうよう

Autumn Colors

In the fall, Japan's mountain-sides blaze
with red- and yellow-leafed trees,
and *momijigari*, or maple-leaf viewing, is
an important seasonal leisure activity.
Like flower-viewing, the custom had its roots
amongst the Heian aristocracy
before spreading to the populace
in the Edo period.
Whereas noblemen and women of old could admire
the autumn colors in their gardens,
modern Japanese are more likely to jump
in a car and head for the countryside.
It is usual to bring home
a few fallen leaves as a souvenir.

MAIN TEXT ― ほんぶん

Look at the picture below and read the following passage.

紅葉
こうよう

日本は 今 紅葉が きれいだ。 木村さんは 今度の 連休に
奥さんと 温泉へ 行って、 紅葉を 楽しもうと 思って いる。
私は 連休に 友だちと 映画を 見て、おいしい 韓国料理を
食べる つもりだ。 好きな 小説も 読みたい。

Autumn Colors
The autumn leaves are lovely at the moment. Mr. Kimura is planning to spend the next long weekend at an *onsen* hot spring resort with his wife and enjoy the fall scenery. I'm going to spend the holiday with my friend, going to the movies and eating some nice Korean food. I also want to read some novels I like.

Listen to and repeat after the tape. High and low pitches are marked with ⌐ and ⌐, and the stressed word is in bold below.

Nihon-wa ima **kooyoo**-ga kiree-da. Kimura-san-wa kondo-no renkyuu-ni okusan-to onsen-e itte, **kooyoo**-o tanoshimoo-to omotte iru. Watashi-wa renkyuu-ni tomodachi-to **eega**-o mite, oishi **Kankoku-ryoori**-o taberu-tsumori-da. Sukina **shoosetsu**-mo yomitai.

EXPLANATION せつめい

The following breakdown of terms will help you to understand the passage.

① 紅葉

こうよう red or yellow leaves

② 日本は　今　紅葉が　きれいだ。

にほん Japan

は as for, speaking of: particle to indicate the topic in the sentence 【→GN❶-4 for the topic particle は】

いま now

が particle to indicate the subject, i.e., what is being talked about in the sentence 【→GN❶-4 for the particle が】

きれい beautiful, attractive: な-adjective 【→GN❶-1, 2 for な-adjective】

だ is, are: copula 【→GN❸-1 for a summary on Japanese predicates】

③ 木村さんは　今度の　連休に　奥さんと　温泉へ　行って、紅葉を　楽しもうと　思って　いる。

きむらさん Mr. Kimura

こんど forthcoming

の of: particle to indicate the noun that modifies a succeeding noun

れんきゅう consecutive holidays, long weekend

に during, at, on, in: here, particle to indicate time

おくさん [someone's] wife

と [together] with: particle

おんせん hot spring [resort]

へ to: particle to indicate direction

いって going: the て-form of いく[to go], here, used to connect sentences

を particle to indicate the [direct] object of the verb 【→ GN❷-1 for the particle を】

たのしもう to intend to enjoy: the -[y]oo form of たのしむ[to enjoy] 【→GN❽-1】

と that: the quotation particle 【→GN❽-1】

おもって いる is thinking: the て いる form of おもう[to think] 【→GN❹-1 for the て／で＋いる／います form】

④ 私は　連休に　友だちと　映画を　見て、おいしい　韓国料理を　食べる　つもりだ。

わたし I

ともだち friend[s]

えいが movie

みて watching: the て-form of みる[to watch], here, used to connect sentences 【→GN❹-1 for the て／で form】

おいしい delicious: い-adjective 【→GN❶-2 for い-adjective】

かんこくりょうり Korean dish: かんこく[Korea]＋りょうり[dish, food]

たべる to eat

つもり intention 【→GN❽-1】

⑤ 好きな　小説も　読みたい。

すきな favorite: な-adjective

しょうせつ novel

も also: particle

よみたい to want to read: the たい-form of よむ[to read] 【→GN❼-2 for the たい／たがっている-form】

DIALOGUE — かいわ

Did you understand the passage? In the following conversation, Ms. Cooper and Mr. Kimura are talking about their holiday plans.

クーパー：いい　季節に　なりましたね。

木村　　：ええ。　今　紅葉が　きれいだそうですよ。

クーパー：今度の　連休の　ご予定は？

木村　　：家内と　近くの　温泉へ　行く　つもりです。　紅葉も　楽しもうと　思って　います。

クーパー：私は　好きな　小説を　たくさん　読む　つもり　です。　そして、友だちと　映画を　見て、おいしい　韓国料理を　食べようと　思って　います。　読書の　秋、食欲の　秋ですから。

Cooper: It's a nice season now, isn't it?

Kimura: Yes, I hear the autumn leaves are lovely at the moment.

Cooper: What are you doing over the next holiday?

Kimura: I'm thinking of going to a nearby *onsen* hot spring resort with my wife. I'd like to see the autumn leaves as well.

Cooper: I'm going to read lots of my favorite novels. Then I'm going to see a movie with a friend and eat some good Korean food. Autumn is the season for reading and eating.

PRONUNCIATION　はつおん

Listen to and repeat after the tape. Try to imitate well when practicing this exercise.

Cooper: **Ii** kisetsu-ni narimashita-ne.

Kimura: Ee. Ima **kooyoo**-ga kiree-da-soo-desu-yo.

Cooper: Kondo-no renkyuu-no **go-yotei**-wa?

Kimura: Kanai-to chikaku-no **onsen**-e iku-tsumori-desu. **Kooyoo**-mo tanoshimoo-to omotte imasu.

Cooper: Watashi-wa sukina **shoosetsu**-o takusan yomu-tsumori-desu. Soshite, tomodachi-to **eega**-o mite, oishii **Kankoku-ryoori**-o tabeyoo-to omotte imasu. **Dokusho**-no aki, **shokuyoku**-no aki-desu-kara.

Did you understand the dialogue? If you didn't, the following breakdown of terms will help you to understand and enjoy it.

⑥いい　季節に　なりましたね。

いい good: い-adjective
きせつ season
に　なりました became: the polite past tense of に　なる
　　[become into...]
ね isn' it true!: particle used at the end of a sentence for
　　confirmation or exclamation

⑦ええ。今　紅葉が
　きれいだそうですよ。

ええ yes: more informal than はい
いま now
そう I hear【→GN❻-1 for a summary on そう】
です copula: the polite form of だ above
よ I tell you, you know: particle used at the end of a
　　sentence for emphasis

⑧今度の　連休の　ご予定は？

の of: particle to indicate the noun that modifies a suc-
　　ceeding noun
ごよてい plan: ご is a prefix to make the following
　　expression more polite

⑨家内と　近くの　温泉へ　行く
　つもりです。

かない [my] wife

ちかく nearby

⑩紅葉も　楽しもうと　思って
　います。

おもって　います is thinking: the polite form of おも
　　って　いる above

⑪私は　好きな　小説を　たくさん
　読む　つもり　です。

たくさん many, much
よむ to read

⑫そして、友だちと　映画を　見て、
　おいしい　アメリカ料理を
　食べようと　思って　います。

そして and: conjunction
たべよう to intend to eat: the -(y)yoo form of たべる
　　[to eat]

⑬読書の　秋、食欲の　秋ですから。

どくしょ reading
あき autumn
しょくよく appetite [for food]
から because: here, conjunction. Both どくしょの　あき
　　and しょくよくの　あき are common expressions
　　to characterize autumn in Japan.

GRAMMAR NOTES (GN❽)
ぶんぽうノート

【GN❽-1】

（1）つもり　だ／です attached to the plain, dictionary form of the verb is usually used for the first person (and for the second person in interrogative sentences) to express one's intention or determination. The negative form is つもりは　ない／ないです／ありません.

来年 ヨーロッパへ 行く つもりだ。 [I] intend to go to Europe next year.

連休に 何を する つもりですか。 What do [you] intend to do during the long weekend?

結婚する つもりは ない。 [I] do not intend to marry.

（2）Similarly, -(y)oo attached to the stem of the verb can indicate one's desire or intention. It is often followed by と(quotation particle)+思う／思います(to think) or 思って　いる／思って　います(to be thinking). The former is used for the first person and the latter can be used for any person.

	example	stem	-(y)oo
-RU ending verb	たべる(tabe-ru)	tabe-	たべよう(tabeyoo)
	みる(mi-ru)	mi-	みよう(miyoo)
-U ending verb	よむ(yom-u)	yom-	よもう(yomoo)
	いく(ik-u)	ik-	いこう(ikoo)

今晩 ビールを 飲もうと 思う／思って いる。
[I] think/am thinking of drinking beer tonight.

山川さんは パソコンを 買おうと 思って いる。
Mr./Ms. Yamakawa is thinking of buying a personal computer.

（3）The quotation particle と(and its colloquial variant って) may be used to quote anything. The plain (dictionary) form of the verb is usually used for indirect quotation.

山川さんは 「パソコンを 買いたいです」と／って 言った。
Mr./Ms. Yamakawa said, "I want to buy a personal computer."

山川さんは パソコンを 買いたいと／って 言った。
Mr./Ms. Yamawaka said that he/she would like to buy a personal computer.

Refer also to sentences ④ ⑨ ⑪ ③ ⑩ ⑫ in the Main Text and the Dialogue.

④私は 友だちと 映画を 見て、おいしい 韓国料理を 食べる つもりだ。

⑨家内と 近くの 温泉へ 行く つもりです。

⑪私は 好きな 小説を たくさん 読む つもりです。

③木村さんは 今度の 連休に 奥さんと 温泉へ 行って、紅葉を 楽しもうと 思って いる。

⑩紅葉も 楽しもうと 思って います。

⑫そして、友だちと 映画を 見て、おいしい アメリカ料理を 食べようと 思って います。

【→Drill 1, 2, Task 1,2】

DRILLS
ドリル

（１）文を　完成させなさい。

Complete the sentences using the words below. 【→GN❽-1, GN❼-2, GN❹-1】

〈クーパさんの決心〉

私は　将来　アメリカへ　帰って、日本語の　教師に（1　　　　　）。　だから、
今　いっしょうけんめいに　日本語の　勉強を（2　　　　　）。　毎日　いろんな
人と　日本語で　話しを（3　　　　）と　思って　いる。　日本語の
テレビ講座も（4　　　　）つもりだ。

〔　（A）しよう　　（B）して　いる　　（C）見る　　（D）なりたい　〕

（２）文を　完成させなさい。

Complete the sentences, changing the given verbs into suitable forms. 【→GN❽-1, GN❼-2】

1　今度の　連休は　どこへ　行きますか。
　→　九州へ　（　　　　　）つもりです。〈行く〉
2　飲物は　何が　いいですか。
　→　コーヒーが　（　　　　）たいです。〈飲む〉
3　何を　食べますか。
　→　ステーキを　（　　　　）ようと　思って　います。〈食べる〉
4　川田さんは　何と　言いましたか。
　→　友だちへ　きのう　手紙を　（　　　　）と　言いました。〈書く〉

VOCABULARY

1

●ぶん = sentence ●かんせいさせなさい = complete: an imperative form of かんせいさせる[to complete] ●けっしん = determination ●しょうらい = [in the] future ●かえって = returning: the て-form of かえる[to return] ●にほんご = the Japanese language ●きょうし = teacher ●だから = therefore: conjunction ●いっしょうけんめいに = very hard ●べんきょう = study ●まいにち = every day ●いろんな = various: な-adjective ●ひと = person ●で = by means of, using: instrumental particle ●はなし = talk ●テレビこうざ = lectures on TV ●しよう = to intend to do: the -[y]oo form of する[to do] ●して いる = is doing: the て いる form of する[to do] ●みる = to watch ●なりたい = to want to become: the たい-form of なる[to become]

2

●どこ = where ●いきます = the polite form of いく[to go] ●か = question particle used at the end of a sentence ●きゅうしゅう = Kyushu: southern island of Japan ●のむ = to drink ●のみもの = drink, beverage ●なに = what ●コーヒー = coffee ●たべます = the polite form of たべる[to eat] ●ステーキ = steak ●かわたさん = Mr./Ms. Kawata ●いいました = the polite past tense of いう[to say] ●きのう = yesterday ●てがみ = letter ●かく = to write

TASKS
タスク

(1) ひとりで 旅行できますか。

Can you travel alone?

【→GN❽-1, GN❼-2】

質問に 答えて ください。

1　新幹線の　「こだま」と　「ひかり」と　「のぞみ」では　どれが　いちばん
　　速いと　思いますか。

(a)「こだま」　　　(b)「ひかり」　　　(c)「のぞみ」

2　「みどりの　窓口」って　何ですか。

(a)きっぷうりば　　(b)ホテルや　旅館の　案内所　　(c)観光バスの　のりば

3　あなたは　たばこが　きらいですね。　どの　車両に　乗る　つもりですか。

(a)寝台車　　　(b)グリーン車　　　(c)禁煙車

4　東京から　京都へ　行く　つもりです。　行きと　帰りの　きっぷが　ほしいです。
　　何と　言いますか。

(a)「東京から　京都まで　往復を　ください。」　　(b)「東京から　京都まで　片道を
ください。」　　(c)「東京から　京都まで　行きと　帰りを　ください。」

いくつ　できましたか。　三つ　以上で　合格です。　あなたは　ひとりで
旅行できます。

(2) ガンバ探偵の 事件メモ❽—本物は どの 人?

The Casebook of Detective Gamba ❽—Who is the Real Person?

【→GN❽-1, GN❼-1, GN❼-2, GN❸-2】

中山さんは 20年ぶりに 息子の 和夫さんに 会って、いっしょに 沖縄旅行を しようと 思いました。 それで、スケジュールを 和夫さんに 送りました。 ところが、出発の 日に 3人の 男の 人が 来ました。 どの 人も 「私が 中山和夫です。」と 言いました。 本当の 中山和夫は どの 人でしょうか。

スケジュール
1日目 羽田空港---〈飛行機〉→那覇空港---〈タクシー〉→ホテル
2日目 レンタカーで 観光地めぐり→万座ビーチ（ダイビング）→ホテル
3日目 〈タクシー〉→那覇空港---〈飛行機〉→石垣島（クルージング）→ホテル
4日目 石垣島→那覇空港→ゴルフ→那覇空港→羽田空港

1 父も 私も 海が 好きです。 2日目に クルージングを して、
　　3日目に およごうと 思って います。
2 父に 会いたかったです。沖縄では 観光地を 見て、その あとは
　　ずっと ゴルフを する つもりです。
3 行きも 帰りも 飛行機ですが、最初は 船で 行く つもりでした。
　　3日目に クルージングを しようと 思って います。

VOCABULARY

1

●ひとりで= alone ●りょこう= travel ●できます= the polite form of できる[can do...] ●しつもん= question ●に こたえて ください= Please answer...: the て-form+ください means a polite request ●しんかんせん= Shinkansen [the bullet train] ●こだま[echo], ひかり[light], のぞみ[hope] are names given to Shinkansen trains. ●と= and: here, particle to list things ●では= among ●どれ= which ●いちばん= to the greatest degree: used here as a superlative【→GN❺-1 for comparative sentences】●はやい= fast: い-adjective ●みどりの まどぐち = みどり[green]の まどぐち[window] is the name of the JR [Japan Railways] ticket window ●きっぷうりば= ticket window ●ホテル= hotel ●りょかん= [Japanese style] inn ●あんないじょ= information desk ●かんこう = sightseeing ●バス= bus ●のりば= stop, stand ●たばこ= tobacco, cigarette ●きらい= to dislike: な-adjective ●ね= you know?: particle used for confirmation ●どの= which __ ●しゃりょう= car ●に のる= to get on..., board...●しんだいしゃ= sleeping car ●グリーンしゃ= first class car ●きんえんしゃ= non-smoking car ●とうきょう= Tokyo ●から= from: particle ●きょうと= Kyoto: ancient capital ●いき= going ●かえり= returning ●ほしい= to want ●いいます= to say: the polite form of いう[to say] ●まで= as far as: particle ●おうふく= round-trip [ticket] ●かたみち= one-way [ticket] ●いくつ= how many ●できました= could do/answer: the past tense of できます[can do] ●みっつ= three [things] ●いじょう= more than ●で= being: the で-form of the copula だ: used here to connect sentences ●ごうかく= passing [an exam] ●あなた= you

2

●たんてい= detective ●じけん= case ●メモ= memo, book ●ほんもの= genuine thing/person ●なかやまさん= Mr./Ms. Nakayama ●にじゅうねんぶりに= after 20 years' absence ●むすこ= son ●かずお= Kazuo: a popular first name for men ●に あって= meeting...: the て-form of に あう[to meet], used here to link sentences ●いっしょに= together ●おきなわ= Okinawa: southern-most islands of Japan ●しよう= to intend to do: the [y]oo form of する[to do] ●それで= then: conjunction ●スケジュール= schedule ●に= to: here, particle to indicate the goal ●おくりました= sent: the polite past tense of おくる[to send] ●ところが= however: conjunction ●しゅっぱつ = departure ●ひ= day ●さんにん= three people ●おとこ= male ●きました= came: the polite past tense of くる[to come] ●どの ひとも+affirmative = every one ●ほんとう= real, true ●でしょう= will probably be: uncertain version of です ●いちにちめ= the first day ●ふつかめ= the second day ●みっかめ= the third day ●よっかめ= the fourth day ●はねだくうこう= Haneda Airport ●なは= Naha: the biggest city in Okinawa ●タクシー= taxi ●レンタカー= rent-a-car ●かんこうち= sightseeing spots ●めぐり= tour ●まんざビーチ= Manza beach ●ダイビング= diving ●いしがきじま= Ishigaki Island ●クルージング= cruising [by boat] ●ゴルフ= golf ●ちち= [my] father ●うみ= ocean ●すき= to like: な-adjective【→GN❼-1 for the use of すき】●して= doing: the て-form of する[to do], used here to link sentences ●およごう= to intend to swim: the-[y]oo form of およぐ[to swim] ●あいたかった= wanted to meet: the past tense of あいたい[to want to meet] ●で= in, at: here, particle to indicate a location where an action takes place ●その あと= after that ●ずっと= all during ●する= to do ●が= but: here, conjunction【→GN❸-2 for the conjunction が】●さいしょ= [at] the beginning ●ふね= ship, boat

⑨ クリスマス
Christmas

The sight of Santa Claus,
snowmen and trees decorating every shop
at least a month before Christmas belies the fact that
the Christmas craze is quite recent,
not even an official holiday
and only a serious religious occasion for
Japan's 3% Christian population.
For most people it is a chance to have fun buying novel gifts,
decorations and food.
For young Japanese, Christmas Eve has become
the most romantic date of the year,
a chance to wine and dine the one you love.
Typical Christmas fare in Japan means take-out fried chicken
and cream-covered sponge Christmas cake.

MAIN TEXT — ほんぶん

Look at the picture below and read the following passage.

クリスマス

もうすぐ　クリスマスだ。　去年の　クリスマスには　金田さんから
日本料理の　本を　もらった。　弟は　クリスマス音楽の　CDを
くれた。　今年は　金田さんに　中華料理の　本を　あげる
つもりだ。　弟には　クリスマスコンサートの　チケットを　買って
やりたい。　山川先生には　何か　お蔵暮を　さしあげようと
思って　いる。

Christmas
It'll soon be Christmas. Last year Mr. Kaneda gave me a book on Japanese cooking. My brother gave me a CD of Christmas music. This year I'm going to give Mr. Kaneda a book on Chinese cooking. I want to buy my brother tickets to a Christmas concert. I'm thinking of giving Professor Yamakawa a year-end gift.

Listen to and repeat after the tape. High and low pitches are marked with ⌐ and ⌐, and the stressed word is in bold below.

Moosugu **kurisumasu**-da. Kyonen-no kurisumasu-ni-wa Kaneda-san-kara **Nihon-ryoori**-no hon-o moratta. Otooto-wa **kurisumasu-ongaku**-no CD-o kureta. Kotoshi-wa Kaneda-san-ni **Chuuka-ryoori**-no hon-o ageru tsumori-da. Otooto-ni-wa **kurisumasu-konsaato**-no chiketto-o katte yaritai. Yamakawa-sensee-ni-wa nanika **oseebo**-o sashiageyoo-to omotte iru.

EXPLANATION せつめい

The following breakdown of terms will help you to understand the passage.

① クリスマス

クリスマス Christmas

② もうすぐ　クリスマスだ。

もうすぐ soon
だ is, are: copula【→GN❸-1 for a summary on Japanese predicates】

③ 去年の　クリスマスには　金田さん
から　日本料理の　本を　もらった。

きょねん last year
の of: particle to indicate the noun that modifies a succeeding noun
に at, on, in: here, particle to indicate time
は as for, speaking of: particle to indicate the topic in the sentence【→GN❶-4 for the topic particle は】
かねださん Mr. Kaneda
から from: particle
にほん Japan[ese]
りょうり cuisine, dish
ほん book
を particle to indicate the [direct] object of the verb【→GN❷-1 for the particle を】
もらった received: the past tense of もらう [to receive]【→GN❾-1 for the giving and receiving verbs】

④ 弟は　クリスマス音楽の　CDを
くれた。

おとうと [my] younger brother
おんがく music
ＣＤ compact disc

くれた gave: the past tense of くれる [to give]

⑤ 今年は　金田さんに　中華料理の
本を　あげる　つもりだ。

ことし this year
に to: here, particle to indicate the goal
ちゅうか Chinese
あげる to give
つもり intention【→GN❽-1 for the つもり だ／です sentence】

⑥ 弟には　クリスマスコンサートの
チケットを　買って　やりたい。

コンサート concert
チケット ticket
かって buying: the て-form of かう [to buy]
やりたい to want to give: the たい-form of やる [to give]【→GN❾-1 for the て+やる form】

⑦ 山川先生には　何か　お歳暮を
さしあげようと　思って　いる。

やまかわせんせい Professor Yamakawa
なにか some[thing]
おせいぼ year-end gift
さしあげよう to intend to give: the -[y]oo form of さしあげる [to give]【→GN❽-1 for the -[y]oo form】
と that: the quotation particle【→GN❽-1 for the quotation particle と】
おもって いる is thinking: the て いる form of おもう [to think]【→GN❹-1 for the て／で+いる／います form】

DIALOGUE — かいわ

Did you understand the passage? In the following conversation, Mr. Kaneda and Ms. Chen are talking about Christmas gifts.

金田：もうすぐ　クリスマスですね。　弟さんに　何か

　　　プレゼントしますか。

陳　：ええ。　クリスマスコンサートの　チケットを　買って

　　　やろうと　思って　います。

金田：ぼくも　ほしいなあ。

陳　：去年は　金田さんに　日本料理の　本を　もらいましたよね。

　　　今年は　私が　中華料理の　本を　あげます。

金田：ぼくは　本より　料理　そのものの　方が　いいです。　本は

　　　山川先生に　さしあげて　ください。

Kaneda: It'll be Christmans soon. Are you going to get your brother anything?
Chen: Yes, I'm thinking of buying him tickets to a Christmas concert.
Kaneda: I wouldn't mind tickets myself.
Chen: You gave me a book on Japanese cookery last year, didn't you? This year I'll give you a book on Chinese cookery.
Kaneda: I'd prefer the real thing rather than a book. Please give the book to Professor Yamakawa.

PRONUNCIATION　はつおん

Listen to and repeat after the tape. Try to imitate well when practicing this exercise.

Kaneda: Moosugu **kurisumasu**-desu-ne. Otooto-san-ni nanika **purezento**-shimasu-ka?

Chen: Ee. **Kurisumasu-konsaato**-no chiketto-o katte yaroo-to omotte imasu.

Kaneda: Boku-mo **hoshii**-naa.

Chen: Kyonen-wa Kaneda-san-ni **Nihon-ryoori**-no hon-o moraimashita-yo-ne.

Kotoshi-wa watashi-ga **Chuuka-ryoori**-no hon o agemasu.

Kaneda: Boku-wa hon-yori **ryoori** sonomono-no hoo-ga ii-desu. Hon-wa **Yamakawa**-sensee-ni sashiagete kudasai.

Did you understand the dialogue? If you didn't, the following breakdown of terms will help you to understand and enjoy it.

⑧ もうすぐ　クリスマスですね。

です is, are: copula, the polite form of だ【→GN❶-1, GN❷-2, for plain vs. polite forms】

ね isn't it!: particle used at the end of a sentence for confirmation or exclamation

⑨ 弟さんに　何か
　プレゼントしますか。

おとうとさん [your/someone's] younger brother

プレゼントします to give a gift, to present: the polite form of プレゼントする[to give a gift]

か question particle used at the end of a sentence

⑩ ええ。クリスマスコンサートの
　チケットを　買って　やろうと
　思って　います。

ええ yes: more informal than はい

やろう to intend to give: the -[y]oo form of やる[to give]

おもって います is thinking: the polite form of おもって いる, see above

⑪ ぼくも　ほしいなあ。

ぼく [masculine] I

も also: particle

ほしい to want【→GN❼-2 for the ほしい sentence】

なあ you know!: an alternate form of ね, often used in men's speech

⑫ 去年は　金田さんに　日本料理の
　本を　もらいましたよね。

に by, from: here, particle to indicate an agent【→GN ❾-1】

もらいました received: the polite past tense of もらう [to receive]

よね particle for emphasis よ+particle for confirmation ね

⑬ 今年は　私が　中華料理の　本を
　あげます。

わたし I

が particle to indicate the subject, i.e., what is being talked about in the sentence【→GN❶-4 for the particle が】

あげます to give: the polite form of あげる[to give]

⑭ ぼくは　本より　料理　そのものの
　方が　いいです。

より [more] than【→GN❺-1 for the comparative sentence with より】

そのもの itself

ほう alternative

いい good: い-adjective【→GN❶-2 for い-adjective】

⑮ 本は　山川先生に　さしあげて
　ください。

さしあげて giving: the て-form of さしあげる[to give]

ください the て-form+ください means a polite request: therefore, さしあげて ください means 'Please give...'

GRAMMAR NOTES (GN❾)

ぶんぽうノート

【GN❾-1】

Giving and Receiving Verbs

（１）There are two sets of giving verbs; やる, あげる, and さしあげる are one set, and くれる and くださる are another set. You should note that くれる and くださる are used only when someone gives something to me (the speaker) or my in-group member(s) such as family members and colleagues. As shown below, やる is usually used when someone, including the speaker, gives to an inferior, あげる when someone gives to an equal, and さしあげる when someone gives to a superior. On the other hand, くれる is used when someone inferior or equal gives to me or my in-group member, and くださる when someone superior gives to me or my in-group member.

Refer to the following sentences in the Main Text and the Dialogue and example sentences.

e.g. 私は 弟に ペンを やった。（←やる）I gave a pen to my younger brother.

⑤今年は 金田さんに 中華料理の 本を あげる つもりだ。（←あげる）

⑬今年は 私が 中華料理の 本を あげます。（←あげる）

⑦山川先生には 何か お歳暮を さしあげようと 思って いる。（←さしあげる）

⑮本は 山川先生に さしあげて ください。（←さしあげる）

④弟は クリスマス音楽の CDを くれた。（←くれる）

e.g. 先生が （私に）本を くださった。（←くださる）[My] teacher gave a book [to me.]

（２）There is only one set of receiving verbs: もらう and いただく. もらう is used when someone, including the speaker, receives from an inferior or an equal, and いただく when someone receives from a superior.

Refer to the following sentences in the Main Text and the Dialogue and an example sentence.

③去年の クリスマスには 金田さんから 日本料理の 本を もらった。（←もらう）

⑫去年は 金田さんに 日本料理の 本を もらいましたよね。（←もらう）

e.g. 私は 先生に／から 本を いただいた。（←いただく）I received a book by/from [my] teacher.

（３）The giving/receiving verbs are often used with the て-form of the verb when an action expressed by the verb involves giving/receiving a favor. The same principles described above also apply here. Refer to the following sentences in the Main Text and the Dialogue and example sentences.

⑥弟には クリスマスコンサートの チケットを 買って やりたい。（←て-form of 買う＋やる）

⑩クリスマスコンサートの チケットを 買って やろうと 思って います。

（←て-form of 買う＋やる）

e.g. 私は 友だちに お金を 貸して あげました。（←て-form of 貸す＋あげる）
I lent [lit. gave a favor of lending] money to [my] friend.

e.g. スミス先生は 私に 英語を 教えて くださいました。（←て-form of 教える＋くださる）
Professor Smith taught [lit. gave a favor of teaching] English to me.

e.g. わたしは 母に 服を 作って もらいました。（←て-form of 作る＋もらう）
My mother made [lit. I received a favor of my mother making] clothes for me.

【→Drill, Task 1, 2】

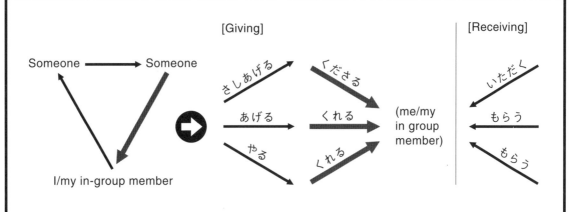

ドリル

文_{ぶん}を 完成_{かんせい}させなさい。

Complete the sentences based on the Main Text and the Dialogue.　　　　　【→GN❾-1】

1　陳_{チェン}さんは　去年_{きょねん}　弟_{おとうと}さんから　クリスマス音楽_{おんがく}の　CDを　（　　　　　）。

2　陳さんは　今年_{ことし}　弟さんに　クリスマスコンサートの　チケットを
　　買_かって　（　　　　　）。

3　陳さんは　今年　山川先生_{やまかわせんせい}に　お歳暮_{せいぼ}を　（　　　　　）。

4　金田さんは　去年　陳さんに　日本料理_{にほんりょうり}の　本_{ほん}を　（　　　　　）。

5　金田さんは　今年　陳さんから　中華料理_{ちゅうか}の　本を　（　　　　　）。

〔　（a）もらう　（b）もらった　（c）あげた　（d）さしあげる　（e）やる　〕

V O C A B U L A R Y

●ぶん = sentence ●かんせいさせなさい = complete: imperative form of かんせいさせる[to complete]

TASKS
タスク

(1) だれが　間違って　いるか。

Who is wrong?　　　　　　　　　　　　　　　　　　　【→GN❾-1, GN❹-1】

　8人の　学生が、下の　図を　見て、日本語の　文を　作りました。　だれが
間違って　いますか。

Aさん：私は　山中さんに　ピアノを　教えて　あげました。
Bさん：私は　結婚式で　中田さんに　写真を　とって　あげました。
Cさん：中田さんは　結婚式で　スミス先生に　スピーチを　して　いただきました。
Dさん：私は　妹に　バッグを　買って　やりました。
Eさん：私は　母に　服を　作って　あげました。
Fさん：山中さんは　私の　妹に　テニスを　教えて　やりました。
Gさん：スミス先生は　私に　英語を　教えて　くださいました。
Hさん：私は　スミス先生に　車で　送って　いただきました。

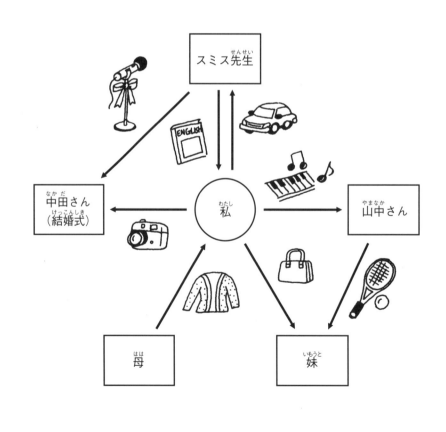

(2) ガンバ探偵の　事件メモ❾―犯人は　だれ？

The Casebook of Detective Gamba ❾—Who is the Criminal?　【→GN❾-1, GN❹-1, GN❸-1】

マンションの　部屋で　会社員の　小川さんが　ナイフで　殺されて　いました。
次の　会話が　小川さんの　テープレコーダーに　残って　いました。
犯人は　だれでしょう。

Pay attention to the difference between the polite form and the non-polite plain form.

？？：ちょっと　話しを　したいけど…

小川：何でしょうか。

？？：あした　会社で　新しい　車の　デザイン会議が　あるね。

小川：はい。　私も　デザインを　発表しようと　思って　います。

？？：その　デザインは　ぼくのだ！　ぼくは　先週　きみに　デザインを　見せて
　　　やった。　そして、きみは　「すばらしい」と　言って　くれた。

小川：はい、　デザインは　見せて　いただきましたが、　私の　デザインは
　　　自分で　考えました！　私の　デザインです！

？？：ちがう！　ぼくのだ！

小川：やめて　ください！　あぶないです！　あぶない！！　あーっ！

大山さん
（会社の　社長）

中村さん
（大学の　後輩）

木村さん
（会社の　上司）

小川さん

本田さん
（会社の　部下）

VOCABULARY

1

●だれ = who ●まちがって いる = to be wrong: the て いる form of まちがう[to make an error] ●はちにん = eight [persons] ●がくせい = student[s] ●した = below ●ず = chart ●みて = looking at: the て-form of みる[to look], used here to link sentences ●にほんご = Japanese language ●つくりました = made: the polite past tense of つくる[to make] ●まちがって います = the polite form of まちがって いる, see above ●やまなかさん = Mr./Ms. Yamanaka ●ピアノ = piano ●おしえて = teaching: the て-form of おしえる[to teach] ●あげました = gave: the polite past tense of あげる[to give] ●けっこんしき = wedding ceremony ●で = at, in: particle to indicate a location where an action takes place ●なかださん = Mr./Ms. Nakada ●しゃしん = photo ●とって = taking [a photo]: the て-form of とる[to get] ●スミスせんせい = Professor Smith ●スピーチ = speech ●して = doing: the て-form of する[to do] ●いただきました = received: the polite past tense of いただく[to receive] ●いもうと = [my] younger sister ●バッグ = bag ●やりました = gave : the polite past tense of やる[to give] ●はは = [my] mother ●ふく = clothes ●つくって = making: the て-form of つくる[to make] ●テニス = tennis ●えいご = English ●くださいました = gave: the polite past tense of くださる[to give] ●くるま = car ●で = by: here, an instrumental particle ●おくって = sending, giving a ride home: the て-form of おくる[to send]

2

●たんてい = detective ●じけん = case ●メモ = memo, casebook ●はんにん = criminal ●マンション = apartment house ●へや = room ●かいしゃいん = かいしゃ[company]+いん[member]●おがわさん = Mr./Ms. Ogawa ●ナイフ = knife ●ころされて いました = was killed: the polite past て いる form of ころされる[to be killed]【→GN⓫-1 for the passive sentence】●テープレコーダー = tape recorder ●のこって いました = remained, was recorded: the polite past て いる form of のこる[to remain] ●でしょう = will probably be: uncertain version of です ●おおやま, きむら, なかむら, ほんだ are all common family names ●しゃちょう = president ●じょうし = boss ●こうはい = one's junior ●ぶか = subordinate personnel ●ちょっと = a little ●はなし = talk ●したい = to want to do: the たい-form of する[to do] ●けど = but: conjunction ●なん = what ●あした = tomorrow ●あたらしい = new: い-adjective ●デザイン = design ●かいぎ = meeting ●ある = there is, to be held ●はい = yes ●も = also: particle ●はっぴょうしよう = to intend to make public/to release: the -[y]oo form of はっぴょうする[to make public] ●その = that __ ●ぼくの = [masculine] mine ●せんしゅう = last week ●きみ = you: typical in men's speech ●みせて = showing: the て-form of みせる[to show] ●やった = gave: the past tense of やる[to give] ●そして = and: conjunction ●すばらしい = splendid: い-adjective ●いって = saying: the て-form of いう[to say] ●が = but: here, conjunction【→GN❸-2 for the conjunction が】●じぶんで = by oneself ●かんがえました = thought: the polite past tense of かんがえる[to think] ●ちがう = no, to be wrong ●やめて ください = please stop: the polite request form of やめる[to stop] ●あぶない = dangerous: い-adjective ●あーっ = ah!, oh!, no!

⑩ 正月
New Year's Day

Perhaps the most important date on
the Japanese calendar,
shoogatsu is a national holiday
when all flights and trains are full of people
returning to their hometowns to
pay respects to ancestors
and pray for good fortune in the coming year.
Hatsumoode, the first shrine visit of the new year,
is a time for women to don kimonos and men suits,
while children receive *o-toshidama*,
a gift of money in a decorative envelope.
Adults and children alike eat carefully prepared and
presented food called *o-sechi ryoori*,
which many think looks nicer than it tastes!

MAIN TEXT — ほんぶん

Look at the picture below and try to read the following passage.

正月

新しい 年に なった。 今年 クーパーさんは 大学を 卒業する。 卒業したら、アメリカへ 帰って、日本語の 先生に なりたいそうだ。 私は 今年 家内と アメリカ旅行を したい。 アメリカへ 行くなら、英会話を 習った ほうが いいが、家内が できるので、私は 習わなくても いい。

New Year's Day

It's the start of a new year. This year Ms. Cooper will graduate from university. I hear she wants to return to the U.S. after graduation to become a Japanese teacher. This year I want to travel to the U.S. with my wife. If we go, I really should study some English, but since my wife speaks English, I don't have to.

Listen to and repeat after the tape. High and low pitches are marked with ⌐ and ⌐, and the stressed word is in bold below.

Atarashii toshi-ni natta.　Kotoshi Kuupaa-san-wa daigaku-o **sotsugyoo**-suru. Sotsugyoo-shitara, Amerika-e kaette, **Nihongo**-no sensee-ni naritai-soo-da.　Watashi-wa kotoshi kanai-to **Amerika-ryokoo**-o shitai. Amerika-e iku-nara, eekaiwa-o naratta-hoo-ga ii-ga, kanai-ga dekiru-node, watashi-wa **narawanakute-mo** ii.

EXPLANATION　せつめい

The following breakdown of terms will help you to understand the passage.

① 正月

しょうがつ New Year's Day, the New Year

② 新しい　年に　なった。

あたらしい new: い-adjective 【→GN❶-2 for い-adjective】

とし year

～に　なった became: the past tense of ～に　なる [to become (into)...]

③ 今年　クーパーさんは　大学を　卒業する。

ことし this year

クーパーさん Ms. Cooper

は as for, speaking of: particle to indicate a topic in the discourse 【→GN❶-4 for the topic particle は】

だいがく college, university

を particle to indicate the [direct] object of the verb 【→GN❷-1 for the particle を】

そつぎょうする to graduate

④ 卒業したら、アメリカへ　帰って、日本語の　先生に　なりたいそうだ。

そつぎょうしたら if [one] graduated: the たら-condition of そつぎょうする above 【→GN❿-1】

アメリカ America, the U.S.

へ to: particle to indicate direction

かえって returning : the て-form of かえる [to return, to go back], used here to link sentences 【→GN❹-1 for the て-form】

にほんご Japanese language

の of: particle to indicate the noun that modifies a suc-

ceeding noun

せんせい teacher

～に　なりたい to want to become: the たい-form of ～に　なる above 【→GN❼-2 for the たい／たがって　いる-form】

そう I hear 【→GN❻-1 for a summary on そう】

だ is, are: copula 【→GN❸-1 for a summary on Japanese predicates】

⑤ 私は　今年　家内と　アメリカ旅行を　したい。

わたし I

かない [my] wife

と together with: particle

りょこう trip, traveling

したい to want to do: the たい-form of する [to do]

⑥ アメリカへ　行くなら、英会話を　習った　ほうが　いいが、家内が　できるので、私は　習わなくても　いい。

いくなら if [you] go: the なら-condition of いく [to go] 【→GN❿-1】

えいかいわ English conversation: えい[English]＋かいわ[conversation]

ならった learned: the past tense of ならう [to learn]

ほう alternative

が particle to indicate the subject of the sentence 【→GN❶-4 for the particle が】

いい good: い-adjective (Note: ～た　ほうが　いい is a suggestion expression meaning 'had better...' 【→GN❿-2】

が but: here, conjunction 【→GN❸-2 for the conjunction が】
できる to be able to [speak]
ので because: conjunction
ならわなくても not learning: the て-form of ならわ

ない[not to learn]+も (Note that い is changed to くて to derive the て-form of い-adjective including ない.)
〜てもいい is a permission expression meaning 'may, it is all right to...' 【→GN❿-2】

DIALOGUE かいわ

Did you understand the passage? In the following conversation, Mr. Kimura and Ms. Cooper are talking about their plans for the new year.

木村　　：明けまして　おめでとう　ございます。

クーパー：明けまして　おめでとう　ございます。

木村　　：クーパーさんは　今年　卒業ですね。　卒業したら、
　　　　　どうしますか。

クーパー：アメリカへ　帰って、日本語の　先生に　なろうと　思って
　　　　　います。　木村さんの　今年の　夢は？

木村　　：家内と　アメリカ旅行を　することです。

クーパー：じゃあ、英会話を　習わなければ　なりませんね。

木村　　：ええ。　でも、英会話は　家内が　できるので、私は
　　　　　習わなくても　いいんです。

Kimura: Happy New Year!
Cooper: Happy New Year!
Kimura: Ms. Cooper, you graduate this year, don't you? What will you do after you graduate?
Cooper: I plan to return to the U.S. and become a Japanese teacher. What would you like to do this year, Mr. Kimura?
Kimura: I'd like to travel to the U.S. with my wife.
Cooper: Well then, you'll have to study some English, won't you?
Kimura: Yes. But my wife speaks English, so I won't have to.

Listen to and repeat after the tape. Try to imitate well when practicing this exercise.

Kimura: Akemashite **omedetoo gozaimasu**.

Cooper: Akemashite **omedetoo gozaimasu**.

Kimura: Kuupaa-san-wa kotoshi **sotsugyoo**-desu-ne. Sotsugyoo-shitara, **doo** shimasu-ka.

Cooper: America-e kaette, **Nihongo**-no sensee-ni naroo-to omotte imasu. Kimura-san-no kotoshi-no **yume**-wa?

Kimura: Kanai-to **Amerika-ryokoo**-o suru-koto-desu.

Cooper: Jaa, **eekaiwa**-o narawanakereba narimasen-ne.

Kimura: Ee. Demo, eekaiwa-wa kanai-ga dekiru-node, watashi-wa **narawanakute-mo** ii-n-desu.

Did you understand the dialogue? If you didn't, the following breakdown of terms will help you to understand and enjoy it.

⑦ **明けまして　おめでとう　ございます。**

あけまして　おめでとう　ございます Happy New Year!

⑧ **クーパーさんは　今年　卒業ですね。**

そつぎょう graduation

です is, are: the polite form of だ above【→GN❶-1, GN❷-2, GN❸-1 for polite vs. non-polite, plain forms】

ね isn't it!: particle used at the end of a sentence for confirmation

⑨ **卒業したら、どうしますか。**

どう how

します to do: the polite form of する[to do]

か question particle used at the end of a sentence

⑩ **アメリカへ　帰って、日本語の　先生に　なろうと　思って　います。木村さんの　今年の　夢は？**

なろう to intend to become: the -[y]oo form of なる[to become]【→GN❽-1 for the -[y]oo form】

と that: the quotation particle【→GN❽-1 for the quotation particle と】

おもって　います is thinking: the polite ている form of おもう[to think]【→GN❹-1 for the て／で+い

る／います form】

ゆめ dream

⑪ **家内と　アメリカ旅行を　することです。**

すること doing: する [to do]+こと[nominalizer used to make a verb into a noun])

⑫ **じゃあ、英会話を　習わなければ　なりませんね。**

じゃあ then: conjunction

ならわなければ　なりません must learn: the polite obligation form of ならう [to learn]【→GN❿-2】

⑬ **ええ。でも、英会話は　家内が　できるので、私は　習わなくても　いいんです。**

ええ yes: more informal than はい

でも but, however: conjunction

んです you know: the polite form of ん／の+だ, which, attached to the plain form of the verb or い-adjective, makes a sentence more colloquial, emphatic, and explanatory (Note: in the case of the noun or な-adjective, なん／なの+だ／です is attached to it.)【→GN❸-1 for a summary on Japanese predicates】

GRAMMAR NOTES (GN⑩)
ぶんぽうノート

【GN⑩-1】

Conditionals: たら／だら and なら. たら／だら is used when realization of what is described in the たら clause is presupposed. The なら clause presupposes a present or future condition, under which one makes a judgment. Refer to the following sentences in the Main Text and the Dialogue:

④ 卒業したら、アメリカへ 帰って、日本語の 先生に なりたいそうだ。

⑨ 卒業したら、どう しますか。

⑥ アメリカへ 行くなら、英会話を 習った ほうが いいが、…

Other conditionals are と and (れ)ば. The と clause indicates a condition that brings about what is described in the main clause. The (れ)ば clause generally presupposes a present or future situation other than those described above. For example:

その 橋を 渡ると、公園が ある。 If you cross the bridge, there is [you'll find] a park.

お金が あれば、中国へ 行きたい。 If I have [enough] money, I'd like to go to China.

Note that たら is the past plain form ～た＋ら; なら and と are attached to the plain form; **(r)eba** is attached to the stem of the verb. 【→ GN❸-1 for the basic verb forms】

【→ Drill 1, Task 2】

【GN⑩-2】

(a) ～なければ ならない(must, have to: obligation) can be derived by changing the negative ない ending to なければ ならない: e.g., 行かない(not to go) → 行かなければ ならない(must go). The polite form is ～なければ なりません.

(b) ～ても／でも いい(may, it is all right to...: permission) is the て／で-form of the predicate＋も いい: e.g., 行く(to go) → 行って → 行っても いい(may go). The polite form is ～ても／でも いいです.

(c) ～ては／では いけない(must not: prohibition) is the て／で-form of the predicate＋は いけない: e.g., 行く(to go) → 行って→ 行っては いけない(must not go). The polite form is ～ては／では いけません.

(d) ～た／だ ほうが いい(had better: suggestion) is the plain, dictionary past tense of the verb+ほうが いい: e.g., 行く(to go) → 行った(went) → 行った ほうが いい(had better go). The polite form is ～た／だ ほうが いいです. 【→GN❸-1, GN❹-1 for different predicate forms】

Refer to the following sentences in the Main Text and the Dialogue and an example sentence:

⑫ じゃ、英会話を 習わなければ なりませんね。

⑥ …… 家内が できるので、私は 習わなくても いい。

⑬ でも、英会話は 家内が できるので、私は 習わなくても いいんです。

e.g. この 水を 飲んでは いけません。 You must not drink this water.

⑥ アメリカへ 行くなら、会話を 習った ほうが いいが、……

【→ Drill 2, Task 1】

DRILLS

ドリル

（１）文を　完成させなさい。

Complete the sentence.　　　　　　　　　　　　　　　　　　　【→GN❿-1】

1　ラーメンを　食べる（　　　）、この　店が　いいです。

2　春に　なる（　　　）、桜が　咲きます。

3　ニューヨークに　着い（　　　）、電話を　ください。

4　この　薬を　飲め（　　　）、よく　なります。

〔　と　　ば　　なら　　たら　〕

（２）文を　完成させなさい。

Complete the sentence.　　　　　　　　　　　　　　　　　　　【→GN❿-2】

1　もう　帰っても　いい　ですか。

　　→いいえ、まだ（　　　　　　）いけません。

2　今日は　働かなくても　いい　ですか。

　　→いいえ、（　　　　　　）なりません。

3　その　試験は　受けなければ　なりませんか。

　　→いいえ、（　　　　　　）いいです。

4　どうして　野菜を　食べないんですか。

　　野菜も　（　　　　　　）ほうが　いいですよ。

V O C A B U L A R Y

1
⬤ぶん＝ sentence ⬤かんせいさせなさい＝ complete: imperative form of かんせいさせる[to complete] ⬤ラーメン＝ ramen: Chinese noodles ⬤たべる＝ to eat ⬤この＝ this ＿ ⬤みせ＝ shop ⬤はる＝ spring ⬤さくら＝ cherry blossom ⬤さきます＝ to bloom: the polite form of さく[to bloom] ⬤ニューヨーク＝ New York ⬤つく＝ to arrive ⬤でんわ＝ phone [call] ⬤ください＝ please give [me] ⬤くすり＝ medicine ⬤のむ＝ to drink, to take ⬤よく＝ well, better

2
⬤もう＝ now, already ⬤いいえ＝ no ⬤まだ＝ yet, still ⬤きょう＝ today ⬤はたらく＝ to work ⬤その＝ that ＿ ⬤しけん＝ exam ⬤うける＝ to take [an exam] ⬤どうして＝ why ⬤やさい＝ vegetable ⬤たべない＝ not to eat: negative form of たべる[to eat]

TASKS
タスク

(1) 日本の 正月—あなたは 何点？
New Year's Day in Japan—What will your score be?

【→GN⑩-2】

正しい ほうを 選んで ください。 1問 20点です。

1 年賀状は

（a）筆で 書かなければ ならない。

（b）筆で 書かなくても いい。

2 友だちの お母さんが 去年 なくなりました。 友だちに

（a）年賀状を 出しては いけない。

（b）年賀状を 出した ほうが いい。

3 年越しそばは

（a）12月31日の 夜 食べた ほうが いい。

（b）1月1日の 朝 食べた ほうが いい。

4 おせち料理に

（a）肉を 使っては いけない。

（b）肉を 使っても いい。

5 初もうでには

（a）着物を 着なければ ならない。

（b）着物を 着なくても いい。

0 〜 40点：もっと 日本語と 日本文化を 勉強しましょう。

 〜 80点：日本の 生活は だいじょうぶです。 ゆっくり 楽しんで ください

 〜100点：あなたは ほとんど 日本人です。

● V O C A B U L A R Y ●

◉にほん= Japan ◉あなた= you ◉なんてん=なん[what, how many]+ てん[point, mark, score] ◉ただしい= correct:い-adjective ◉えらんで ください= please choose: the polite request form of えらぶ[to choose] ◉ねんがじょう= New Year's card ◉ふで= brush ◉で= with, by: an instrumental particle ◉かく= to write ◉ともだち= friend ◉おかあさん= [someone's] mother ◉きょねん= last year ◉なくなりました= died: the polite past tense of なくなる[to die, to disappear] ◉に= to, for: particle to indicate a goal/purpose ◉だす= to send ◉としこしそば= New Year's Eve buckwheat noodles ◉じゅうにがつ= December ◉さんじゅういちにち= 31st ◉よる= [at] night ◉いちがつ= January ◉ついたち= 1st ◉あさ= [in the] morning ◉おせちりょうり= New Year's dishes, food ◉にく= meat ◉つかう= to use ◉はつもうで= the year's first visit to shrines/temples ◉きもの= kimono ◉きる= to wear ◉もっと= more ◉ぶんか= culture ◉べんきょうしましょう= let's study: the polite let's form of べんきょうする[to study] ◉せいかつ= life ◉だいじょうぶ= all right, secure ◉ゆっくり= leisurely ◉たのしんで ください= please enjoy: the polite request form of たのしむ[to enjoy] ◉ほとんど= almost

(2) ガンバ探偵の　事件メモ ❿ ─誘拐事件

The Casebook of Detective Gamba ❿ —An Abduction Case 　　　　　　　　　　　　【→GN❿-1】

女の　子が　誘拐されました。
女の　子の　お父さんは　犯人の　手紙を
ガンバ探偵に　見せました。
ガンバ探偵は　お金を　持って　いかなければ
なりません。どの　ビルへ　行けば
いいでしょうか。

犯人の　手紙

花山駅の　前を　まっすぐ　行くと、
橋が　ある。　その　橋を
渡らないで、　左へ　行くと、
もう　一つ　橋が　ある。　その
橋を　渡ると、右に　美術館、左に
公園が　ある。　公園を　左へ
まがると、小さい　ビルが　ある。
子どもを　助けたいなら、その
ビルへ　1000万円　持って　こい。
もし、警察に　話したら、
子どもを　殺す。

VOCABULARY

●たんてい = detective ●じけん = case ●メモ = memo, casebook ●ゆうかい = kidnapping, abduction ●おんなのこ = girl ●ゆうかいされました = was kidnapped: the polite passive past tense of ゆうかいする[to kidnap]【→GN⓫-1 for the passive sentence】●おとうさん = [someone's] father ●はんにん = criminal ●てがみ = letter ●みせました = showed: the polite passive past tense of みせる[to show] ●おかね = money ●もって いく = to take ●どの = which ●ビル = building ●でしょう = will probably be: uncertain version of です ●はなやまえき = Hanayama Station ●まえ = front ●を = through: here, particle to indicate a location where some motion takes place ●まっすぐ = straight ●はし = bridge ●ある = there is, to exist ●わたらないで = without crossing: the negative form of わたる[to cross]+で ; ～ないで means 'without doing ～' ●ひだり = left ●もう ひとつ = one more ●みぎ = right ●びじゅつかん = art museum ●こうえん = park ●まがる = to turn ●ちいさい = small: い-adjective ●こども = child[ren] ●たすけたい = to want to save: the たい-form of たすける[to save] ●いっせんまんえん = 10 million yen ●もって こい = bring: strong imperative form of もって くる[to bring] ●もし = if ●けいさつ = police ●はなす = to talk, to speak ●ころす = to kill

⑪ 節分
<ruby>せ<rt></rt></ruby>

Setsubun

Held on February 3 or 4,
this is one of many rites held
to ward off evil.
In a custom called *mamemaki*,
soybeans are scattered inside and
outside the house to
the chant of
'*Oni wa soto, fuku wa uchi*'
('Out with demons-in with good luck!')
Traditionally,
family members have to eat
the same number of beans as their age,
which might be difficult
for Japan's many octogenerians!

MAIN TEXT — ほんぶん

Look at the picture on the next page and read the following passage.

節分 (せつぶん)

今日は　節分だ。　朝　若宮神社の　豆まきへ　行った。　豆まきの
行事は　とても　おもしろかったが、人が　おおぜい　いて、何度も
足を　踏まれた。　帰りに　豆を　たくさん　買ったので、今晩　弟に
鬼の　役を　やらせて、豆まきを　しようと　思って　いる。

Setsubun

Today is Setsubun. In the morning, I went to a bean-throwing ceremony at Wakamiya Shrine. It was very interesting, but there were so many people there that I had my feet stepped on many times. On my way home, I bought lots of beans, so tonight I'm going to perform *mamemaki* with my brother as the demon.

PRONUNCIATION　はつおん

Listen to and repeat after the tape. High and low pitches are marked with ⌐ and ¬ , and the stressed word is in bold below.

Kyoo-wa **setsubun**-da. Asa Wakamiya-jinja-no **mamemaki**-e itta. Mamemaki-no gyooji-wa totemo **omoshirokatta**-ga, hito-ga oozee ite, nando-mo ashi-o **fumareta**. Kaeri-ni **mame**-o takusan katta-node, konban otooto-ni oni-no yaku-o yarasete, **mamemaki**-o shiyoo-to omotte iru.

EXPLANATION　せつめい

The following breakdown of terms will help you to understand the passage.

① 節分

せつぶん Setsubun, the beginning of spring in the old lunar calendar

② 今日は　節分だ。

きょう today

は as for, speaking of: particle to indicate the topic in the sentence 【→GN❶-4 for the topic particle は】

だ is, are: copula 【→GN❸-1 for a summary on Japanese predicates】

③ 朝　若宮神社の　豆まきへ　行った。

あさ [in the] morning

わかみやじんじゃ Wakamiya Shrine

の of: particle to indicate a noun that modifies a succeeding noun

まめまき bean-throwing [ceremony on the day of Setsubun]

へ to: particle to indicate direction

いった went: the past tense of いく [to go]

④豆まきの　行事は　とても
　おもしろかったが、人が　おおぜい
　いて、何度も　足を　踏まれた。

ぎょうじ event
とても very
おもしろかった was interesting, enjoyable: the past
　　tense of い-adjective おもしろい【→GN❶-2,
　　GN❸-1 for い-adjective and its past tense】
が but: here, conjunction【→GN❸-2 for the con-
　　junction が】
ひと person, people
が particle to indicate the subject, i.e., what is being
　　talked about in the sentence【→GN❶-4 for the
　　particle が】
おおぜい many [people]
いて there being: the て-form of いる[to exist], used here
　　to link sentences【→GN❹-1 for the て-form】
なんども many times
あし foot, feet
を particle to indicate the [direct] object of the verb【→
　　GN❷-1 for the particle を】
ふまれた was stepped on: the passive past tense of ふ
　　む[to step on]【→GN⓫-1】

⑤帰りに　豆を　たくさん
　買ったので、今晩　弟に　鬼の　役を
　やらせて、豆まきを　しようと
　思って　いる。

かえりに on the way back
まめ bean[s]
たくさん many, much
かった bought: the past tense of かう[to buy]
ので because: conjunction
こんばん tonight
おとうと [my] younger brother
に here, particle to indicate the agent【→GN⓫-1】
おに devil, demon
やく role
やらせて making [one] do: the て-form of the causative
　　of やる[to do]【→GN⓫-1】
しよう to intend to do: the -[y]oo form of する[to do]
　　【→GN❽-1 for the -[y]oo form】
と that: the quotation particle【→GN❽-1 for the
　　quotation と】
おもって いる is thinking: the て いる form of おも
　　う[to think]【→GN❹-1 for the て／で＋いる／
　　います form】

DIALOGUE ― かいわ

Did you understand the passage? In the following conversation, Ms. Chen and Mr. Kaneda are talking about the bean-throwing ceremony on the day of Setsubun.

陳　：けさ　若宮神社の　豆まきへ　行って　きました。

金田：そうですか。　どうでしたか。

陳　：とても　おもしろかったです。　でも、人が　おおぜい　いて、
　　　何度も　足を　踏まれました。

金田：それは　ちょっと　たいへんでしたね。　ところで、その　豆は
　　　どう　するんですか。

陳　：今晩　弟に　鬼の　役を　やらせて、豆まきを　しようと
　　　思って…。

金田：よかった。　ぼくが　やらせられるかと　思いました。

Chen: I went to a bean-throwing ceremony at Wakamiya Shrine this morning.
Kaneda: Really? How was it?
Chen: It was very interesting. But there were so many people there, and my feet were stepped on many times.
Kaneda: Hmm, that wasn't very pleasant for you. By the way, what are you going to do with the beans?
Chen: I was thinking of getting my brother to be the demon and doing my own bean-throwing this evening.
Kaneda: Good–I thought you were going to ask me to be the demon!

Listen to and repeat after the tape. Try to imitate well when practicing this exercise.

Chen: Kesa Wakamiya-jinja-no **mamemaki**-e itte kimashita.

Kaneda: **Soo**-desu-ka. **Doo**-deshita-ka.

Chen: Totemo **omoshirokatta**-desu. Demo, hito-ga oozee ite, nando-mo ashi-o **fumaremashita**.

Kaneda: Sore-wa chotto **taihen**-deshita-ne. Tokorode, sono **mame**-wa doo suru-n-desu-ka.

Chen: Konban otooto-ni oni-no yaku-o yarasete, **mamemaki**-o shiyoo-to omotte …

Kaneda: Yokatta. **Boku**-ga yaraserareru-ka-to omoimashita.

EXPLANATION　せつめい

Did you understand the dialogue? If you didn't, the following breakdown of terms will help you to understand and enjoy it.

⑥けさ　若宮神社の　豆まきへ　行って　きました。

けさ this morning
いって きました went [and came back]: the polite past tense of いって くる [to go and come back]【→GN❶-1,GN❷-2,GN❸-1 for polite vs. plain forms】

⑦そうですか。どうでしたか。

そうですか Is that so?
どう how
でした was: the polite past tense of だ above
か question particle used at the end of a sentence

⑧とても　おもしろかったです。でも、人が　おおぜい　いて、何度も　足を　踏まれました。

です here, copula to make おもしろかった above a more polite expression
でも but: conjunction
ふまれました was stepped on: the polite form of ふまれた above

⑨それは　ちょっと　たいへんでしたね。

それ that
ちょっと a little
たいへん awful, terrible: な-adjective【→GN❶-2 for な-adjective】

ね isn't it?: particle used at the end of a sentence for confirmation

⑩ところで、その　豆は　どう　するんですか。

ところで by the way
その that __
する to do
んです the polite form of of ん／の＋だ, which, attached to the plain form of the verb or い-adjective, makes a sentence more colloquial, emphatic, and explanatory. In the case of the noun or な-adjective, なん／なの＋だ／です is attached to it.

⑪今晩　弟に　鬼の　役を　やらせて、豆まきを　しようと　思って…。

おもって thinking: the て-form of おもう [to think]

⑫よかった。ぼくが　やらせられるかと　思いました。

よかった Good! I feel relieved!: the past tense of い-adjective いい [good]
ぼく [masculine] I
やらせられる to be forced to do: the causative-passive of やる [to do]【→GN⑪-1】
おもいました thought: the polite past tense of おもう [to think]

GRAMMAR NOTES (GN⓫)
ぶんぽうノート

【→GN⓫-1】

The passive, the causative, and the causative-passive.

（１） The passive verb basically means 'to be affected by an action or state,' and is derived by adding -(r)are-ru [plain]/masu [polite] to the stem of the verb, whether it is transitive or intransitive. The agent that affects someone/something is marked with に in the passive sentence. 【→GN❸-1 for the basic verb forms】

（私は） 子どもに 泣かれた。

(nak-u → nak-are-ru → nak-are-ta) [I] was affected by my child crying.

子どもは 先生に ほめられました。

(home-ru → home-rare-masu → home-rare-mashita) [My] child was praised by the teacher.

④…何度も 足を 踏まれた。

(fum-u → fum-are-ru → fum-are-ta) See the Main Text. Note that the direct object, here 足を, remains as it is in the passive sentence.) 【→Drill (A), Task 2】

（２） The causative verb basically means 'to cause [let/make] someone or something to do something,' and is derived by adding -(s)ase-ru [plain]/masu [polite] to the stem of the verb.

私は 子どもを／に 買物に 行かせます。

(ik-u → ik-ase-masu) I'll make/let my child go shopping. (Note that the を causative is generally coercive, i.e., 'make' causative, and the に causative is permissive, i.e.,'let' causative, when the verb is intransitive.)

私は 子どもに さしみを 食べさせた。

(tabe-ru → tabe-sase-ru → tabe-sase-ta) I made/let my child eat sashimi [raw fish].

(Whether the causative sentence with the transitive verb is coercive or permissive depends on the context.)

⑤…今晩 弟に 鬼の 役を やらせて、……

(yar-u → yar-ase-ru → yar-ase-te)(See the Main text.) 【→Drill (B), Task 1】

（３） The causative-passive verb always means 'to be made/forced to...,' and is derived by adding -(s)ase-rare-ru [plain]/masu [polite] to the stem of the verb.

⑫ぼくが やらせられるかと 思いました。

(yar-u → yar-ase-rare-ru) (See the Dialogue.)

ドリル

下の　動詞を　（A）受身形、（B）使役形に　変えて、文を　完成させなさい。

Change the following verbs into their passive (A) and causative (B) forms and complete the sentences.

【→GN⓫-1】

（A）けさ　8時に　母に（　　　　　　　）た。　すぐ　学校へ　行ったが、遅刻したので、先生に（　　　　　　　）た。　友だちにも（　　　　　　　）た。

〔　からかう(to tease)　しかる(to scold)　起こす(to wake someone up)　〕

（B）夕食の　後　母は　わたしに　あとかたずけを（　　　　　　　）た。　私は妹に（　　　　　　　）た。　弟には　犬の　散歩に（　　　　　　　）た。

〔　手伝う(to help, to give a hand)　する(to do)　行く(to go)　〕

● ● ● V O C A B U L A R Y ● ● ●

●した = below ●どうし = verb ●うけみけい = passive form ●しえきけい = causative form ●～に　かえて = changing into: the て-form of ～に　かえる[to change into...] ●ぶん = sentence ●かんせいさせなさい = complete: an imperative form of かんせいさせる[to complete] ●はちじ = eight o'clock ●に = at, on: here, particle to indicate time ●はは = [my] mother ●すぐ = soon ●がっこう = school ●ちこくした = was late: the past tense of ちこくする[to be late] ●せんせい = teacher ●ともだち = friend[s] ●も = also: particle ●ゆうしょく = supper, dinner ●あと = after ●あとかたずけ = clearing up, cleaning up ●いもうと = [my] younger sister ●おとうと = [my] younger brother ●いぬ = dog ●さんぽ = walk ●に = for: here, particle to indicate purpose

TASKS
タスク

(1) あなたは どんな お母さん／お父さん？

What kind of mother/father will you be? 　　　　　　　　　　【→ GN⑪-1, GN⑩-1】

あなたに 赤ちゃんが 生まれたら、どんな 育て方を しますか。

Yes ⟶／No ➡ で 答えて ください。

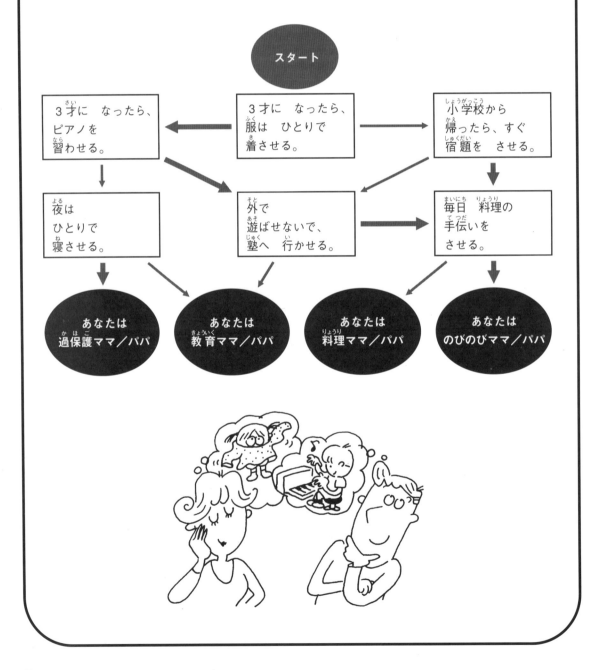

スタート

| 3才に なったら、ピアノを 習わせる。 | 3才に なったら、服は ひとりで 着させる。 | 小学校から 帰ったら、すぐ 宿題を させる。 |

| 夜は ひとりで 寝させる。 | 外で 遊ばせないで、塾へ 行かせる。 | 毎日 料理の 手伝いを させる。 |

あなたは 過保護ママ／パパ

あなたは 教育ママ／パパ

あなたは 料理ママ／パパ

あなたは のびのびママ／パパ

(2) ガンバ探偵の　事件メモ⓫—木田さんの　うそ

The Casebook of Detective Gamba ⓫—Mr. Kida's Lie 　　　　　　【→GN⓫-1】

ある日　木田さんの　部屋に　どろぼうが　入りました。
（A）は　その　前の　日、（B）は　その　次の　日の
木田さんの　部屋です。　ガンバ探偵は　木田さんの
話を　聞きました。　そして、うそを　一つ
見つけました。　さて、木田さんが　どろぼうに
とられなかった　物は　何でしょう。

木田さんの　話
ガンバ探偵、助けて　ください。　きのう　どろぼうに
入られたんです。　窓ガラスを　割られて、いろんな　物を　盗ま
れました。　絵と　パソコンと　ラジオを　盗まれました。　そう
そう　カメラも　かばんも　とられました。

（A）

（B）

1

●あなた = you ●どんな = what kind of ●おかあさん = mother ●おとうさん = father ●に = with: here, a relational particle ●あかちゃん = baby ●うまれたら = if [a baby] were born: the たら-condition of うまれる [to be born] 【→GN❿-1 for conditionals】●そだてかた = how to raise ●します = to do: the polite form of する[to do] ●で = with, by: here, an intrumental particle ●こたえて ください = please answer: the polite request form of こたえる [to answer] ●スタート = start ●さんさい = three years old ●に なったら = if [you] became/turned: the たら-condition of ～に なる[to become...] ●ふく = clothes ●ひとりで = by oneself ●きさせる = to make/let [one] wear: the causative of きる[to wear] ●しょうがっこう elementary school ●から = from ●かえったら = if [one] returned: the たら-condition of かえる [to return] ●しゅくだい = homework ●させる = to make/let [one] do: the causative of する[to do] ●ピアノ = piano ●ならわせる = to make/let [one] learn: the causative of ならう[to learn] ●よる = [at] night ●ねさせる = to make/let [one] sleep: the causative of ねる[to sleep, to go to bed] ● そと = outside ●で = at, in: here, particle to indicate a location where an action takes place ●あそばせない = not to make [one] play: the negative causative of あそぶ[to play] ●～ないで = without doing...●じゅく = private cram school ●いかせる = to make/let [one] go: the causative of いく[to go] ●まいにち = every day ●りょうり = cooking ●てつだい = help ●かほご = overprotecting, pampering ●ママ = mom, mother ●パパ = dad, father ●きょういく = education: きょういくママ means a pushy mother when it comes to education ●のびのび = free and easy

2

●たんてい = detective ●じけん = case ●メモ = memo, casebook ●きださん = Mr./Ms. Kida ●うそ = lie ●ある ひ = one day ●へや = room ●どろぼう = thief ●はいりました = entered, broke in: the polite past tense of はいる[to enter, to break in] ●まえ = before ●ひ = day ●つぎ = next ●はなし = talk, story ●ききました = listened to: the polite past tense of きく[to listen to] ●そして = and: conjunction ●ひとつ = one ●みつけました = found: the polite past tense of みつける[to find] ●さて = well ●とられなかった = was not stolen, was not taken: the negative past passive of とる[to take, to steal] ●もの = thing, object: Note that もの is modified by a preceding clause ending with とられなかった.●なん = what ●でしょう = will probably be: uncertain version of です ●たすけて ください = please help: the polite request form of たすける[to help] ●きのう = yesterday ●はいられた was entered, was broken in: the past passive of はいる above ●まど = window ●ガラス = glass ●わられて = being broken: the て-form of the passive of わる[to break] ●いろんな = many kinds of: な-adjective ●ぬすまれました = was stolen: the polite past passive of ぬすむ[to steal] ●え = picture ●と = and: particle ●パソコン = personal computer ●ラジオ = radio ●そうそう = oh, yes! I remember! ●カメラ = camera ●かばん = bag ●とられました = was stolen, was taken away: the polite past passive of とる, see above

⑫ 卒業
そつぎょう

Graduation

Graduation from junior high school signals
change for young Japanese.
Since many will be going on to different high schools
and saying goodbye to old friends,
it is an emotional occasion.
For parents, particularly mothers,
it is a chance to wear their best clothes and feel proud.
The graduation ceremony usually takes
place in the school gym hall,
where students and their parents sit and listen to speeches
by people like the local mayor and the school principal.
Then they go up one by one to receive
their graduation certificates.
The ceremony usually ends with a rousing song.

MAIN TEXT — ほんぶん

Look at the picture on the next page and read the following passage.

卒業

いよいよ　卒業だ。　卒業後は　アメリカへ　帰って、日本語の
教師に　なる　つもりだ。　これまで　いろいろな　方、特に　長野
先生に　たいへん　お世話に　なった。　長野先生は　夏に　学会で
アメリカへ　いらっしゃるそうだ。　ぜひ　また　お会い　して、
専門の　お話しを　お聞き　したい。

Graduation

I'll be graduating soon. Afterwards I plan to go back to the United States and become a teacher of Japanese. I've had a tremendous amount of help from various people, especially Professor Nagano. It looks like Professor Nagano will be going the U.S. in the summer for an academic conference. I'd really like to meet him again and hear his expert advice.

PRONUNCIATION　はつおん

Listen to and repeat after the tape. High and low pitches are marked with ⌐ and ¬, and the stressed word is in bold below.

Iyoiyo **sotsugyoo**-da. Sotsugyoo-go-wa America-e kaette, **Nihongo**-no kyooshi-ni naru tsumori-da. Kore-made iroirona kata, tokuni **Nagano-sensee**-ni taihen osewa-ni natta. Nagano-sensee-wa **natsu**-ni gakkai-de America-e irassharu-soo-da. Zehi mata **oai** shite, semmon-no ohanashi-o **okiki** shitai.

EXPLANATION ·　せつめい

The following explanation of terms will help you to understand the passage.

① 卒業

そつぎょう graduation

② いよいよ　卒業だ。

いよいよ at last, finally

だ is, are: copula 【→GN❸-1 for a summary on Japanese predicates】

③ 卒業後は　アメリカへ　帰って、
　　日本語の　教師に　なる　つもりだ。

ご after

は as for, speaking of: particle to indicate the topic in the sentence 【→GN❶-4 for the topic particle は】

アメリカ America

へ to: particle to indicate direction

かえって returning back: the て-form of かえる[to return, to go back]【→GN❹-1 for the て-form】

にほんご Japanese [language]

の of: particle to indicate the noun that modifies a succeeding noun

きょうし teacher: a formal term to describe one's occupation as a teacher

〜に なる to become...

つもり intention【→GN❽-1 for intentional expressions】

④これまで いろいろな 方、特に 長野先生に たいへん お世話に なった。

これまで until now

いろいろな various: な-adjective【→GN❶-2 for な-adjective】

かた person: an honorific equivalent of ひと[person]【→GN⓬-1】

とくに especially

ながのせんせい Professor Nagano

に by, from: here, particle to indicate an agent or a source

たいへん very [much]

おせわに なった received [kind] assistance: the honorific past tense of せわに なる[to receive assistance]

⑤長野先生は 夏に 学会で アメリカへ いらっしゃるそうだ。

なつ summer

に in, on, at: here, particle to indicate time

がっかい academic conference

で because of, due to: here, particle to indicate a weak cause

いらっしゃる to go, to come, to be: the honorific form of いく[to go], くる[to come], or いる[to exist]【→GN⓬-1】

そう I hear【→GN❻-1 for a summary on そう】

⑥ぜひ また お会い して、専門の お話しを お聞き したい。

ぜひ really, by all means

また again

おあい して meeting: the て-form of the humble form of あう[to meet]【→GN⓬-1】

せんもん speciality

おはなし talk: the honorific form of はなし【→GN⓬-1】

を particle to indicate the [direct] object of the verb

おきき したい to want to hear: the たい-form of the humble form of きく[to hear, to listen to]【→GN⓬-1, GN❼-2 for the たい／たがって いる-form】

DIALOGUE かいわ

Did you understand the passage? Following is the conversation between Professor Nagano and one of his students, Ms. Cooper, on the day of her graduation.

長野　　：クーパーさん、卒業　おめでとう。

クーパー：ありがとう　ございます。　いろいろ　お世話に

　　　　　なりました。

長野　　：帰国して、日本語の　先生に　なるそうだね。

クーパー：はい。　がんばって、いい　教師に　なりたいと　思って

　　　　　おります。

長野　　：夏に　学会で　アメリカへ　行くので、その　時に　また

　　　　　会えるかもしれないね。

クーパー：そうですか。　ぜひ　お会い　したいです。

　　　　　よろしかったら、その　時に　私の　家にも　遊びに

　　　　　いらっしゃって　ください。

Nagano: Ms. Cooper, congratulations on your graduation.
Cooper: Thank you. You've been very kind to me.
Nagano: I hear you're going to become a Japanese teacher when you go home.
Cooper: Yes. I'll try my best to become a good teacher.
Nagano: I'm going to the United States for a conference in the summer, so we might be able to meet again then.
Cooper: Really? I'd like to meet up. I'd be honored if you came to my house.

Listen to and repeat after the tape. Try to imitate well when practicing this exercise.

Nagano : Kuupaa-san, sotsugyoo **omedetoo**.

Cooper : Arigatoo gozaimasu. Iroiro **osewa**-ni narimashita.

Nagano : Kikoku-shite, **Nihongo**-no sensee-ni naru-soo-da-ne.

Cooper : Hai. Gambatte, **ii** kyooshi-ni naritai-to omotte orimasu.

Nagano : Natsu-ni gakkai-de America-e iku-node, sono toki-ni mata **aeru**-
        kamoshirenai-ne.

Cooper : Soo-desu-ka. Zehi **oai** shitai-desu. Yoroshikattara, sono toki-ni watashi-
        no **ie**-ni-mo asobi-ni irasshatte kudasai.

EXPLANATION   せつめい

⑦クーパーさん、卒業　おめでとう。

おめでとう Congratulations!

⑧ありがとう　ございます。
　　いろいろ　お世話に　なりました。

ありがとう ございます Thank you.
いろいろ in various ways: here, adverb. See いろいろ
　　な above.
おせわに なりました received [kind] assistance: the
　　polite form of おせわに なった above.【→GN❶-
　　1,GN❷-2,GN❸-1 for polite vs. pain forms】

⑨帰国して、日本語の　先生に
　　なるそうだね。

きこくして returning to one's country: the て-form of
　　きこくする [to return to one's country]
せんせい teacher
ね isn't it?: particle used at the end of a sentence for
　　confirmation

⑩はい。がんばって、いい　教師に
　　なりたいと　思って　おります。

はい yes
がんばって trying hard: the て-form of がんばる [to
　　try hard]
いい good: い-adjective【→GN❶-2 for い-adjective】
〜に　なりたい to want to become: the たい-form of
　　〜に なる [to become...]
と that: the quotation particle【→GN❽-1 for the
　　quotaion particle と】
おもって おります is thinking: the polite humble て
　　いる form おもう [to think]【→GN⓬-1, GN❹-1
　　for the て／で＋いる／います form】

⑪夏に　学会で　アメリカへ
　　行くので、その　時に　また　会える
　　かもしれないね。

いく to go
ので because: conjunction
その ときに at that time: その [that]＋とき [time]＋に [at]
あえる can meet: the potential form of あう [to meet]
　　(The potential form is derived by adding [rar] e-ru
　　to the stem of the verb.)
かもしれない might

⑫そうですか。ぜひ　お会い
　　したいです。

そうですか Is that right!
おあい したいです to want to meet: the polite humble
　　たい-form of あう [to meet]【→GN⓬-1】

⑬よろしかったら、その　時に　私の
　　家にも　遊びに　いらっしゃって
　　ください。

よろしかったら if you like: the たら-condition of よ
　　ろしい, the polite equivalent of いい [good]【→
　　GN⓾-1 for conditionals】
わたしの my
いえ home, house
に to: here, particle to indicate direction
も also: particle
あそび play, pleasure
に for: here, particle to indicate purpose
いらっしゃって ください please come: the polite request
　　form of いらっしゃる, the honorific form of くる [to
　　come], いく [to go], or いる [to exist]【→GN⓬-1】

GRAMMAR NOTES (GN⓬)
ぶんぽうノート

【GN⓬-1】
Honorific and Humble Forms

（１） Honorific forms are used to exalt the position of the subject when the subject deserves respect from the speaker, and are never used in reference to oneself.
Productive honorific forms: (i) お ～ に　なる[plain]／なります[polite] is attached to the bound (i.e., ます-dropped) form of the verb, or (ii) -(r)are-ru [plain]/masu[polite], which is the same as the passive suffix 【→GN⓫-1】, is attached to the stem of the verb. (Note that the polite ます [or です] form is used when the speaker is expected to be polite to the listener.)

話す(to talk):　┌→ **hanashi**(masu) → o + **hanashi** + ni naru/narimasu
　　　　　　　└→ **hanas**(u) + (r)are-ru/masu → **hanas**-are-ru/masu

You should memorize non-productive lexical honorific forms such as:
いらっしゃる／いらっしゃいます(←いる[to exist], 行く[to go], 来る[to come]) めしあがる／めしあがります(←食べる) おっしゃる／おっしゃいます(←言う[to say]) なさる／なさいます(←する[to do]) ごらんに　なる／ごらんに　なります(←見る[to see])

Honorific forms of some nouns and adjectives can be derived by attaching the prefix お or ご like: お手紙 (letter), ご研究(research), おいそがしい(busy), ご親切(kind)

（２） Humble forms are used when the speaker or his/her in-group member wishes to talk humbly without exalting the position of the subject.
Productive humble forms: お ～ する[plain]／します[polite] is attached to the bound form of the verb.

待つ(to wait): **machi**(masu) → o + **machi** + suru/shimasu

You should memorize non-productive lexical humble forms such as:
おります(←いる[to stay]) まいります(←行く[to go], 来る[to come]) いただく／いただきます(←食べる[to eat]) いたします(←する[to do])

Refer to the honorific and humble expressions in the Main Text and the Dialogue:
⑤長野先生は　夏に　学会で　アメリカへ　いらっしゃるそうだ。
⑬よろしかったら、その　時に　私の　家にも　遊びに　いらっしゃって　ください。
⑥ぜひ　また　**お会い**　して、専門の　**お話し**を　**お聞き**　したい。
⑩がんばって、いい　教師に　なりたいと　思って　**おります**。
⑫ぜひ　**お会い**　したいです。　　　　　　　　　　　　　　　　　　　　【→Drill, Task 1, 2】

ドリル

正しい 方を 選びなさい。

Choose the correct verb forms.

【→GN⓬-1】

山川先生を （1　お招きに　なって　2　お招き　して）、きのう　同窓会を
行いました。　私たちは　駅で　先生を　（1　お待ちに　なりました　2　お待ち
しました）。　先生は　奥さまと　ごいっしょに　（1　いらっしゃいました
2　まいりました）。　私たちは　20年ぶりに　先生に　（1　お会いに　なりました
2　お会い　しました）。　先生は　たくさん　お酒を　（1　めしあがりながら
2　いただきながら）、いろいろな　ことを　（1　お話しに　なりました
2　お話しししました）。　先生の　お話に　私たちは　みんな　（1　感動なさいました
2　感動いたしました）。

●ただしい = right: い-adjective ●ほう = alternative ●えらびなさい = choose: an imperative form of えらぶ[to choose] ●やまかわせんせい = Professor Yamakawa ●まねく = to invite ●きのう = yesterday ●どうそうかい = reunion ●おこないました = did, held: the polite past tense of おこなう[to do, to hold] ●わたしたち = we ●えき = station ●で = in, at, on: particle to indicate a location where an action takes place ●まつ = to wait ●おくさま = [someone's] wife: the honorific equivalent of おくさん ●ごいっしょに = together with: the honorific form of いっしょに ●にじゅうねんぶりに = after 20 years' absence ●たくさん = much, many ●おさけ = sake, liquor: the polite expression of さけ ●めしあがりながら = while drinking/eating: めしあがり, the bound form of honorific めしあがる[to eat, to drink]+ながら[while] ●こと = thing[s] ●おはなし = talk: the honorific form of はなし ●みんな = all ●かんどうする = to be moved/impressed

TASKS
タスク

(1) 教授（助教授、講師、助手）は　だれだ？

Who is the professor (assistant professor, lecturer, assistant)?

【→GN⓬-1】【→GN❾-1】【→GN❿-2】【→GN❹-1】

山田、中本、小川、木村は　教授、助教授、講師、助手の　名前です。　だれが
教授で、だれが　助教授で、だれが　講師で、だれが　助手でしょうか。　会話を
よく　読んで　ください。

小川：中本先生、先週　謝恩会の　はがきを　お送り　したんですが、ご都合は
　　　いかがでしょうか。

中本：出席する　つもりだけど。　山田先生は　出席されるのかな。　もうすぐ
　　　イギリスへ　行くと　おっしゃって　いたけど。

小川：山田先生からは　ご出席の　ご返事を　いただきました。　でも、木村先生は
　　　出席されないそうです。

中本：そうか。　木村先生は　最近　体調が　悪いらしい。　早く　病院へ
　　　行ったほうが　いいと　言ったんだけどね。

---

1 教授（　　　）

2 助教授（　　　）

3 講師（　　　）

4 助手（　　　）

(2) ガンバ探偵の　事件メモ ⓬ ─殺された　時間は？

The Casebook of Detective Gamba ⓬—What Time was he Killed?

【→GN⓬-1】【→GN⓫-1】【→GN❹-1】

会社の　社長が　殺されました。
奥さんと　秘書と　運転手の
話しを　聞いて、
何時から　何時の　間に　殺されたか
考えて　ください。

奥さん：主人は　6時半に　帰宅いたしました。　食事の　後、
7時半には　書斎で　仕事を　して　おりました。　わたしは
用事で　8時に　出かけて、11時に　帰って　まいりました。
そしたら、主人が…。

秘書：社長は　お昼から　ゴルフに　おいでに　なって、4時に
会社に　お帰りに　なりました。　それから　会議に　出席されて、
6時に　帰宅されました。　8時半ごろ　次の　日の
予定について　電話で　お話し　いたしましたが、それっきり…。

運転手：6時半に　お宅まで　お送り　しましたが、車の　中に
書類を　お忘れに　なったので、9時に　お宅に　お届け　しました。
あの　ときは　まだ　お元気でした。

1

●きょうじゅ = professor ●じょきょうじゅ = assistant professor ●こうし = lecturer ●じょしゅ = assistant ●だれ = who ●が = particle to indicate the subject, i.e., what is being talked about in the sentence【→GN❶-4 for the particle が】●やまだ, なかもと, おがわ, きむら are all common family names. ●なまえ = name ●で = being: derived from だ and used here to connect sentences ●でしょう = will probably be: uncertain version of ですか = question particle ●よく well ●よんで ください = please read: the polite request form of よむ[to read] ●せんしゅう = last week ●しゃおんかい = thank-you party for the teachers ●はがき = postcard ●おおくり した = sent: the humble past tense of おくる[to send] ●んです = you know: the polite form of ん／の＋だ, which, attached to the plain form of the verb, makes a sentence more colloquial, emphatic, and explanatory ●が = but: here, conjunction ●ごつごう = convenience: the honorific form of つごう ●いかが = how: more polite than どう[how] ●しゅっせきする = to attend ●けど = but: conjunction ●しゅっせきされる = to attend: the honorific form of しゅっせきする[to attend] ●のかな = I wonder if... ●もうすぐ = soon ●イギリス = England ●おっしゃって いた = was saying: the honorific past て いる form of いう[to say] ●ごしゅっせき = attendance: the honorific form of しゅっせき ●ごへんじ = reply: ご is a prefix to make へんじ more polite ●いただきました = received: the polite past tense of いただく【→GN❾-1 for giving and receiving verbs】●でも = but: conjunction ●しゅっせきされない = not to attend: the negative form of しゅっせきされる above ●そうか = Is that right!: the non-polite form of そうですか above ●さいきん = recently ●たいちょう = physical condition ●わるいbad: い-adjective ●らしい = it seems that ●はやく = promptly ●びょういん = hospital ●いった ほうが いい = had better go【→GN❿-2 for related expressions】

2

●たんてい = detective ●じけん = case ●メモ = memo, casebook ●ころされた = was killed: the past passive of ころす[to kill]【→GN⓫-1 for the passive sentence】●じかん = time ●かいしゃ = company ●しゃちょう = president ●ころされました = was killed: the polite form of ころされた above ●おくさん = [someone's] wife ●と = and ●ひしょ = secretary ●うんてんしゅ = chauffeur ●きいて = listening to: the て-form of きく[to listen to] ●なんじ = what time ●から = from ●あいだ = during ●かんがえて ください = please think: the polite request form of かんがえる[to think] ●しゅじん = [my] husband ●ろくじはん = 6:30 ●きたくいたしました = returned home: the polite humble form of きたくする[to return home] ●しょくじ = meal ●あと = after ●しちじはん = 7:30 ●しょさい = study ●しごと = work ●して おりました = was doing: the humble form of して いました ●わたし = I ●ようじで = on business ●はちじ = eight o'clock ●でかけて = going out: the て-form of でかける[to fo out], used here to connect sentences ●じゅういちじ = eleven o'clock ●かえって まいりました = came back: the humble form of かえって きました[come back] ●そしたら = then ●おひる = noon ●ゴルフ = golf ●おいでに なって = going: the て-form of honorific おいでに なる[to go, to come, to exist] ●よじ = four o'clock ●おかえりに なりました = returned: the polite past tense of honorific おかえり になる[to return] ●それから = after that ●かいぎ = meeting, conference ●しゅっせきされて = attending: the て-form of honorific しゅっせきされる[to attend] ●きたくされました returned home: the polite past tense of honorific きたくされる[to return home] ●ごろ = about, around ●つぎ = next ●ひ = day ●よてい = schedule ●に ついて = about, concerning ●でんわで = on the phone ●おはなし いたしました = talked: the very polite past tense of humble おはなし する[to talk] ●それっきり = that was the last... ●おたく = house: the honorific equivalent of いえ[house] ●まで = as far as, until ●おおくり しました drove one back: the polite past tense of humble おおくり する[to escort] ●くるま = car ●なか = inside ●しょるい = papers ●おわすれに なった = forgot: the past tense of honorific おわすれに なる[to forget] ●おとどけ しました = took: the polite past tense of humble おとどけ する[to take] ●あの とき = [at] that time ●まだ = still, yet ●おげんきでした was fine/well: the honorific past tense of げんきです[is fine]

ANSWERS

DRILLS
ドリル

❶ 1 これは大きい木だ。／この木は大きいです。

2 その花はきれいだ。／それはきれいな花です。

3 あれはにぎやかなまちだ。／あのまちはにぎやかです。

4 そのほんはあたらしい。／それはあたらしいほんです。

❷ (2) 1 だれもきません。　2 何もありません。　3 何もたべません。　4 どこへも行きません。

❸ (1) 1 行った　2 見た　3 いた　4 おもしろかった　4 話した　5 書いた

(2) 1 c　2 d　3 b　4 a

❹ 1 しています　2 のんでいます　3 着ています　4 うっています　5 持っています

❺ (1) 1 広い　2 大きい　3 重くない　4 長くない　5 古い

(2) ① 低い-⑥ 高い　② すずしい-⑨ あたたかい　③ むずかしい-⑧ やさしい

④ まずい-⑩ おいしい　⑤ すくない-⑦ 多い

❻ (1) 1 はれ　2 強い　3 しずか　4 天気だ

(2) 1 (b)　2 (d)　3 (c)　4 (a)

❼ (1) 1 陳さん　2 金田さん　3 じょうずだ　4 したがっている

(2) 1 ためたい　2 行きたい　3 教えたい　4 結婚したい　5 住みたい

❽ (1) 1 (D)　2 (B)　3 (A)　4 (C)

(2) 1 行く　2 飲み　3 食べ　4 書いた

❾ 1 (b)　2 (e)　3 (d)　4 (b)　5 (a)

❿ (1) 1 なら　2 と　3 たら　4 ば

(2) 1 帰っては　2 働かなければ　3 受けなくても　4 食べた

⓫ (A) 起こされ／しかられ／からかわれ

(B) させ／手伝わせ／行かせ

⓬ 2／2／1／2／1／1／2

ANSWERS

TASKS
タスク

❶ (1) 1 b 2 d 3 a 4 c

(2) ⑦

❷ (2) ん

❸ (1) 1 C 2 D 3 B 4 A

(2) F

❹ (1) 1 かけてある 2 しめている 3 おいてある 4 つけてある 5 しめてある

(2) 山田^{やまだ}さん A 小林^{こばやし}さん G 中川^{なかがわ}さん B

1.いいえ 2.はい 3.いいえ 4.はい 5.はい 6.いいえ

❺ (1) (B)

(2) ⑤

❻ (1) 花子^{はなこ}さん 札幌^{さっぽろ} 雪子^{ゆきこ}さん 大阪^{おおさか}

(2) (a) 3 (b) 7 (c) 11 (d) 1 (e) 5 (f) 9 (g) 2 (h) 6 (i) 10 (j) 4 (k) 8 (l) 12

❼ (1) A-E B-C (2) 佐藤^{さとう}さん

❽ (1) 1 (c) 2 (a) 3 (c) 4 (a)

(2) 3

❾ (1) Eさん／Fさん／Hさん (2) 木村^{きむら}さん

❿ (1) 1 (b) 2 (a) 3 (a) 4 (b) 5 (b)

(2) A

⓫ (2) カメラ

⓬ (1) 1 山田^{やまだ} 2 中本^{なかもと} 3 木村^{きむら} 4 小川^{おがわ}

(2) 9時^{くじ}〜 11 時^{じゅういちじ}